P9-DNW-839

REAL STORIES. REAL ADVENTURES. REAL SIGNIFICANCE.

The Second Half

H|T®

TABLE OF CONTENTS

THE SECOND HALF
BY LLOYD REEB

Halftime
2626 Cole, Suite 900
Dallas, TX 75204
www.halftime.org

Created by Lloyd Reeb in cooperation with the people telling their stories. Produced by Lloyd Reeb.

HALF | TIME®
Success to Significance®

A Halftime Book
www.halftime.org/thesecondhalf

CHAIRMAN
Bob Buford

PRESIDENT/CEO
Tom Wilson

MANAGING DIRECTOR OF HALFTIME
Tiger Dawson

First Edition: August 2008
ISBN: 978-0-615-25251-3
Book design by DOXA

Printed in the U.S

"...captivating stories to spawn meaningful "second half" conversations with your spouse." **Lloyd Reeb**

FOREWORD

Many of you are reaching a point in life when the pursuit of material success no longer is enough. You want the second half of your life to count for something bigger than yourself ... something significant. This pause in life is often called Halftime – a time to look back and take stock, a time to look forward and dream, and a time to chart a new course with those you love.

Over the past decade I have traveled the world helping others on this journey from success to significance. I made a Halftime transition myself more than a dozen years ago, and I've written books and curriculum about this perplexing journey. And, yet, by probing deep inside the hearts of the men and women in this book, I learned something profound from each of them. I think you will, too.

These folks stand out in our culture not because of their talent, success or fame, but because they looked inside and found what they are most passionate about, listened carefully for their unique calling and then summoned the courage to live it out. So as we study their lives, we see models of how rewarding the second half can be.

Many of you will reach Halftime and struggle to find the words to share what's happening in your heart with those you love. So how can you show them the kind of life you envision? One way is through stories – real stories that become even more powerful when surrounded by captivating images that make them come alive.

Some of these stories flow out of compassion, while many flow out of compassion mixed with sincere faith – perhaps a blend of compassion, faith and adventure. You know better than anyone what blend of compassion, faith and adventure drives you on this quest, and I hope these stories ignite a spark that helps propel you from dreams to action.

As you read, you are welcome to visit www.halftime.org/thesecondhalf and learn more about each person, listen to parts of my conversations with them, explore their ministry online and even link up with them directly.

There are some questions at the end of the book that I hope you will discuss with your spouse or those around you whose lives will be impacted by your choices. My wife Linda and I have talked with many couples in Halftime. One of the most important things you can do is to listen carefully to each other's dreams and support each other as they take shape. HT

Sincerely,

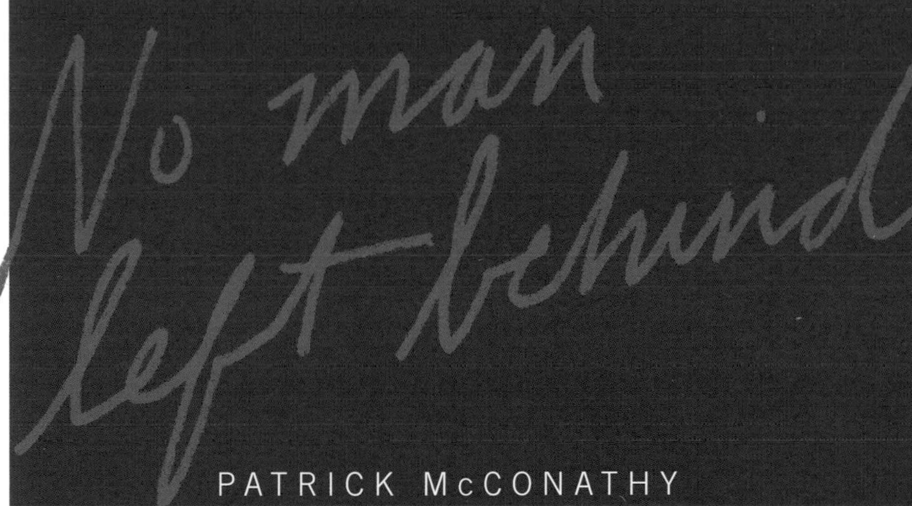

PATRICK McCONATHY

My friend Patrick McConathy never saw it coming, but then, his life's been a series of such unexpected surprises. Patrick is a cowboy at heart – a risk-taker to the point of recklessness. Unexpected surprises come with the territory.

He had achieved considerable success in the oil and gas business, but he never expected to go bankrupt. And after he more than remade the wealth he'd lost, he never expected to turn the ranch he bought near Vail, Colo., into a place that's healing the hearts of men.

So he certainly never expected the most significant 10 days of his life to begin by listening to a group of teen-age boys talk around a campfire on a clear August evening.

Talking faster than I could write as he shared this experience with me, I could tell he was still exhausted but exhilarated.

"I guess I'll always talk about this week until there is another one like it, because it just encompasses so many things," Patrick says. "It was by far the most important week of my life."

Most weeks of the year, Patrick and his ministry partner, Randy Simmonds, welcome a group of men to the ranch for a journey that they hope will help heal their hearts and, through this healing, heal their families. So when Patrick's brother-in-law asked to bring his band of nine 13-year-old boys to HorizonQuest, it seemed like a poor fit. The ranch caters to small groups of men, usually no more than five. Plus, HorizonQuest already planned to depart from its normal routine that week, and Patrick didn't need any additional challenges. On the same day the teens would leave, Patrick would welcome in a group of high-profile leaders and then help later in the week with a group of 16 recently disabled veterans.

By reluctantly allowing the use of the ranch for teens, however, he was about to find out how abandoning his own plans could lead to moments of great significance. The day after the boys arrived, he found himself sitting near them at the fire pit as his brother-in-law asked a penetrating question: What is it that you're afraid of?

"These boys started going around the circle talking about what they were afraid of, (and) it was the same things 50 year old guys are afraid of – the same things," he says. "They're afraid of their dad, not being good enough, not going to heaven, afraid of God, afraid of snakes, whatever. But man, it was just like adults. I'm crying, because it just hit me. Unbelievable."

The difference is that these boys have a mentor who is committed to helping them identify their fears, wounds and disappointments and handle them in a healthy way.

Patrick committed to having the boys back to the ranch each summer until they graduated from high school, but his week of surprises was only beginning. His next group included retired general Hal Moore, championship football coach Bill Curry and several prominent businessmen. Patrick was supposed to lead them in a discussion about spiritual leadership, and he had low expectations. He'd never led such a discussion. Unlike most groups who came to the ranch, most of these men didn't already know each other. And while they all were successful, they had extremely diverse political views and backgrounds.

Despite their differences, these leaders bonded quickly. And not only did they benefit from the time together, they later

"These boys started going around the circle talking about what they were afraid of, (and) it was the same things 50 year old guys are afraid of – the same things."

realized how powerfully they would be used to encourage and inspire the veterans and their families who were arriving later.

This was the vets' first trip away from the Walter Reed Hospital after extensive rehabs – a time to rest while also trying some of the many ranch activities and, in so doing, rebuilding their confidence.

When Greg, a former college football star now a double above-the-knee amputee, rolled up in his wheelchair, he shouted, "Hey Coach." Bill Curry turned to see the boy he knew when he coached at the University of Alabama. He knew his position, his number, even his name. "The last game this boy had played at West Point, defensive end, was against the University of Alabama in the Sun Bowl," Patrick says. "They relived every play."

So, when Greg decided later that week that he didn't want to try horseback riding, Coach Curry had the relationship to roll him away and ask, "Greg, I can think of many reasons you would not want to ride, but tell me what's going through your mind." Greg was direct in his reply: "I just want to sit straight in the saddle."

Patrick was watching this unfold and sensing that something incredible, even sacred, was happening on his ranch. "Doesn't everybody want to sit straight in life?" Patrick says. "You can write a book about sitting straight."

With encouragement and assistance from Coach Curry, Greg sat straight.

A final twist during the week came when Gen. Moore, best known by many because his story was told in the 2002 movie *We Were Soldiers*, spoke to the veterans. Patrick had asked that he talk about something other than his military experiences, figuring it would be nice to

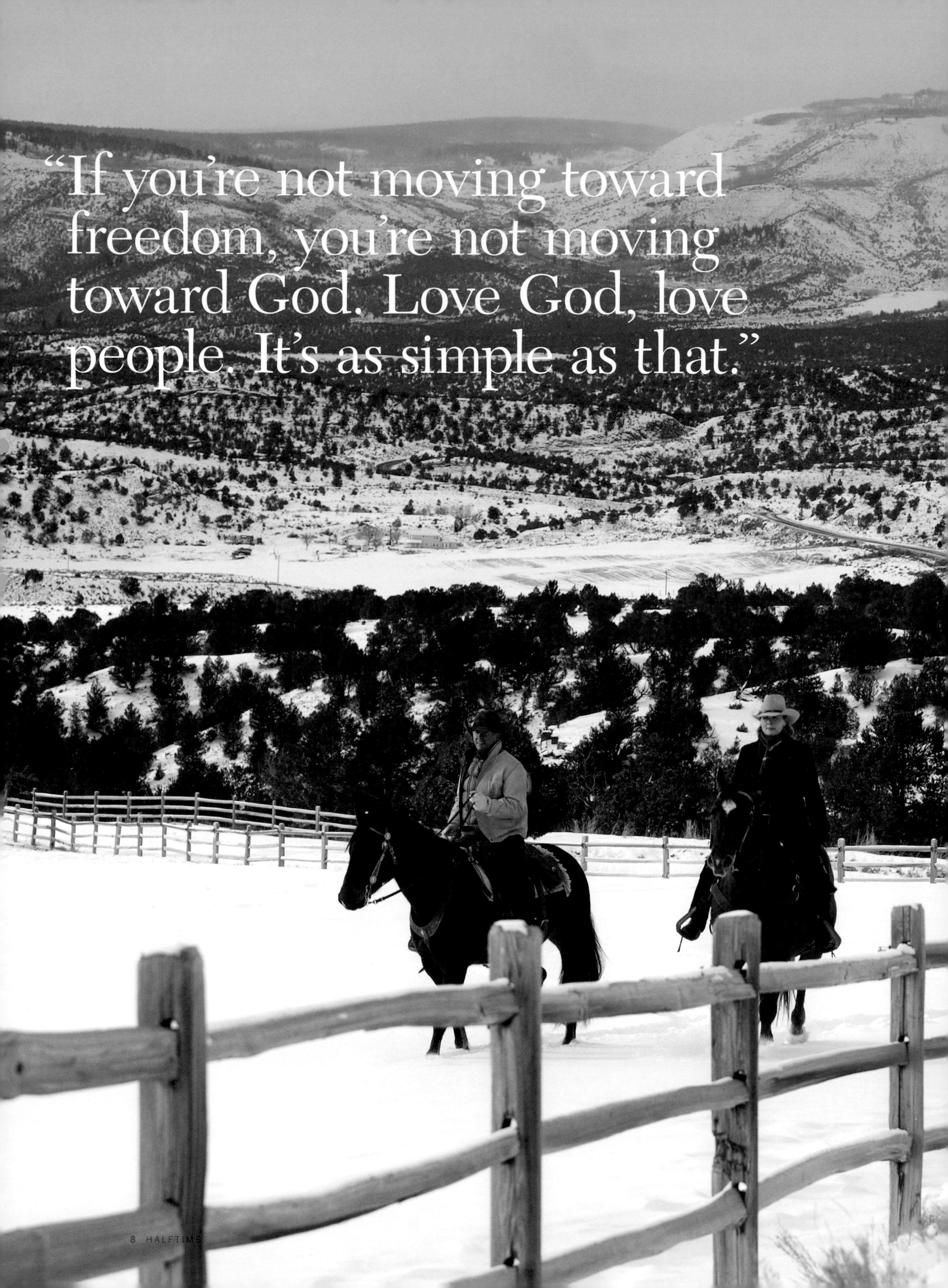

"If you're not moving toward freedom, you're not moving toward God. Love God, love people. It's as simple as that."

hear about different areas of his life. At the last minute, however, Patrick asked another guest to introduce Moore, and that guest encouraged Moore to talk about his military experiences.

"He talked about his love for the men, and he talked about all the things I didn't want him to talk about, which turned out to be exactly the right thing," Patrick says. "Gen. Moore got up there, and he talked about war, and he talked about love, and he talked about spirituality, and he talked about never quitting. … It was great, but I tell you that to say I was so wrong. Everything that seemed wrong to me turned out to be the right way."

The powerful week sums up Patrick's journey of unexpected twists and turns. And they are all leading to something bigger and better than he'd ever envisioned. What he now sees as his second-half calling wasn't born out of a longing to do something more significant with his life, but from following each turn until he ended up where he is today.

He moved his family to Vail, Colo., when it became clear his sons had the talent to compete against the world's best in snow skiing. And he bought the sprawling ranch in the Rocky Mountains because his wife dreamed of a country home where she could garden and ride horses. During a blessing ceremony for the home on the ranch, a friend gave him a copy of *Wild at Heart* by John Eldredge, and Patrick soon began to understand the need to help men explore their deepest fears, share their greatest joys and develop meaningful bonds with each other.

Patrick gave away hundreds of copies of Eldredge's book, and men inevitably called to talk through what they were reading. They'd open up about their deepest issues, and he'd open up about his. Most had similar fears and scars, he discovered. So he renovated an existing 1896 ranch house and partnered with his friend Randy Simmonds to start HorizonQuest as a way for such men to discover God's freedom.

"If you're not moving toward freedom, you're not moving toward God," he says. "Love God, love people. It's as simple as that."

The lodge has produced a constant stream of inspiring stories, Patrick says, not least of which is his unlikely friendship with Gen. Moore – Patrick a former wartime protester and Moore a wartime hero.

"When I introduce him, the only thing that's mandatory that I say is that he's most proud of the fact that he was always the first man on the battlefield, as it says in the movie, and the last one off, and he never left a man behind, dead or alive," Patrick says.

"Well that's what we try to do at the lodge. Men get together and leave no one behind on the battlefield, not after divorce, not after whatever is happening in their life, they stick together." HT

For additional information and helpful Web links related to Patrick's journey from success to significance, visit www.halftime.org/thesecondhalf and click on his name.

Permission for passion

ROSALIND COOK

Rosalind Cook sneaks up on you – at least she did to me. Rosalind spoke several years ago at a Halftime event I was leading in Tulsa, and she came across as a soft-hearted woman with amazingly kind eyes.

What sneaks up on you is that she has world-class talent that she wields strategically, not only as a successful businessperson but also to make an immense impact for the causes she cares deeply about. So I hope she and her art will sneak up on you, as well.

Rosalind was at an art show once when a man fixed his attention on two of her bronze sculptures, one depicting Noah and the other a boy holding a frog, studying each other with delight.

"Why would you do something like this," he said as he pointed to the boy with the frog, "when you can do something as spiritual as this?" And he pointed to the sculpture of Noah.

For Rosalind, the man had missed a huge point with her work. "Can't you see," she told him, "this is a spiritual moment — the boy and the frog discovering each other and the wonder of the creation?"

"When someone
feels God's call,
you've got to
recognize it was
God that put that
passion in you."

"The man just didn't get it," she told me. I think he just wasn't open to being snuck up on.

In a way, it took some time for Rosalind's talent to sneak up on her, as well. She has turned a first-half hobby and frustration into a second-half career and ministry, but only after giving herself "permission," as she puts it, to fully embrace the passion she has for art.

"When someone feels God's call, you've got to recognize it was God that put that passion in you," she says. "And then it's a big step for most women, just giving ourselves permission to move out in it. … All of our lives we've served other people, and when you find a passion, for some reason you think it's a little selfish. So you've got to give yourself permission. When you don't give yourself permission, you're saying to God, 'You must be making a mistake here. You must have made a mistake picking me to give this passion to, this joy, because I'm not worthy.'"

Rosalind, who was born in Lima, Peru, developed a love for different people and cultures while living the first seven years of her life in an isolated community in the Andes. Her passion for people and her awareness for shapes and forms developed even more during her early professional career as a teacher in a school for the blind.

She began sculpting in the 1970s while pregnant with the first of her three children, and she recognized her passion for art the first time she sank her hands into a mound of clay. "Shaping that clay into a meaningful form was like finding a piece of myself that had been missing for a long, long time," she says.

But life was busy, and for years she considered her sculpting merely a hobby. She kept busy as a stay-at-home mother of three, along with all the work she did in the community, schools, and her church activities.

Then one evening a missionary friend saw tears brim in her eyes as she pulled out her clay. "I don't understand how I can have so much joy in doing this!" she told him. "Where's the significance? This isn't saving souls. This isn't doing anything for anyone. It just feeds me and brings me joy."

Her friend's words changed her life: "Rosalind, you are made in God's image," he said. "He's your Creator, and when you use the gifts of His image, that gives Him pleasure."

"From that day on, I gave myself permission to sculpt," says Rosalind. "And I finally connected with its true significance in my life. I was 41. I cast my first bronze at 42 and was able to sell it almost immediately."

"From that day on, I gave myself permission to sculpt. And I finally connected with its true significance in my life."

Since then, Rosalind's work has been in high demand at galleries around the country and as commissioned work at hospitals, parks, libraries, churches, corporate headquarters and private homes. Many of her works are used in fund-raisers for a variety of charities.

"Look at the joy I've had and the fulfillment, and also helping other people's lives," she says. "That's been so exciting for me. That's the most exciting part."

Rosalind's works have proven the power of art to impact people at the point of their deepest need. For instance, a woman who leads a group for parents whose children have committed suicide uses one of her smaller pieces, "Breaking Free."

"She purchased the piece to use in their discussions on breaking free of guilt," Rosalind says. "Another woman – I've got little notes on people – she had gone through a terrible divorce and was left with absolutely nothing after having everything. She said, 'I'm just breaking free of the bitterness and the anger of that, and I'm starting my new life.' I think a painting or a sculpture is a tangible point, a tangible means of seeing God's intangible miracles just like in love stories."

"So many people live with regrets because they don't give themselves permission," she adds. "They don't see how it breaks God's heart when He puts these opportunities and gifts in our life, and we don't use them, and nurture them, and grow them, and share them. Then we look back with regret. … I want to know I've lived life well, that I've used, and nurtured, and grown, and shared the things in my life."

Before you leave this story I want you to take a close look at the photos of the life-size sculpture of Jesus playing with kids – it was being unveiled at the new Children's Hospital at Saint Francis in her hometown of Tulsa. What you can't see from these photos is that this sculpture was carefully designed to be just as compelling when viewed from, say a third-floor window, as it is when you walk up to the main entrance. She had in mind a little boy or girl who might spend weeks or months looking out those hospital windows, and each day seeing in this sculpture God's love and compassion. Go see it for yourself. It will sneak up on you. HT

For additional information and helpful Web links related to Rosalind's journey from success to significance, visit www.halftime.org/thesecondhalf and click on her name.

a joint partnership

CLIFF AND ROSE RATKOVICH

It was a balmy night for an outdoor party in Newport Beach, Calif., as about a dozen Halftime-type couples mingled on the back patio of a French Country home with quiet music, fresh hors d'oeuvres and warm conversation.

I was standing to the side, almost in the shadows, because at the core I am somewhat shy. When I have a choice, I'd rather chat with one person about real issues than several people about the weather. But I wasn't alone for long. Cliff Ratkovich walked over with intentionality in his step: "I know what I want to do with my second half, Lloyd, but I am not exactly sure how it will all work."

After listening to what he had in mind, it seemed like a great idea. So I said, "I like to sail, Cliff, and one thing I know is that you can't steer a sailboat if it's tied to the dock. So, why don't you cut the lines and lift your sails and see where God takes you?" I'm not sure where I got that piece of "wisdom" or even if it was

RELAX

particularly wise advice, but he took it.

As president of a division of one of the largest home-building companies in California, his life had been all about seeing an opportunity, buying the land and getting something built. But he was slow to set sail with his second-half adventure, despite the encouragement of his wife.

Rose Ratkovitch is a strong, professional woman and a leader in her own right. And when she returned from visiting family in Minnesota to discover her husband had found a new passion in life, she embraced a dream that would change her world forever.

Cliff's idea for using his "real estate development gifts" to serve people in poor living conditions came as he approached his 50th birthday. One Saturday morning after reading a book about using your talents "the light bulb really came on" and Cliff had an idea. Unable to focus on anything else, he wrote out a detailed plan for a nonprofit that would remodel homes for the underprivileged in Orange County, Calif.

"I just rolled out of bed, went right to the computer, turned it on, and hammered out a ministry vision," he says. "It was one of those situations where the words just flowed, and I stayed there until I finished it. I went back and read it, and said there's nothing I need to change here. This is going to work."

Rose, whose professional background is restaurant operations and marketing with Coca-Cola, knew from the minute she heard the plan that she wanted to be involved.

"God, I think, just said this is right, and I felt that it was right because of the gifts I know I have," she says. "I'm very relational. I love communication. I love getting people together. I think I have that gift of hospitality. So I saw this ministry really as an extension of that, as a way to serve others. It was just serving a product I had never served, which was housing."

So not long after the party in Newport Beach, Cliff and Rose set sail with HopeBuilders Global. And Cliff's grandiose, not to mention unfunded, dream put the couple on a course that's taken them across the globe together. With Cliff serving as president and Rose as marketing director, it took only a few years to amass almost 1,000 volunteers in their database. From that organization grew the Tapestry Homes Initiative, a project that addresses housing needs for the extreme poor in other parts of the world.

"Maybe I was naïve in not thinking far enough along, but I just felt we could do this," Rose says. "It was something that God had equipped both of us to do, and as a team we could do it."

Most couples don't end up working side-by-side in their second-half projects, of course, but Rose points out that those couples still need to support each other's Halftime efforts 100 percent, even if one of them stays home with the children or works a different job or with other nonprofits.

Cliff and Rose are like many Halftimers in that, while they have been successful, they are not financially independent.

"The thought had occurred to me that you really are not in a position to retire, so maybe you should postpone this tugging at your heart and jumping into your Halftime moment," Cliff recalls. "But what struck me was if you don't do it now, when

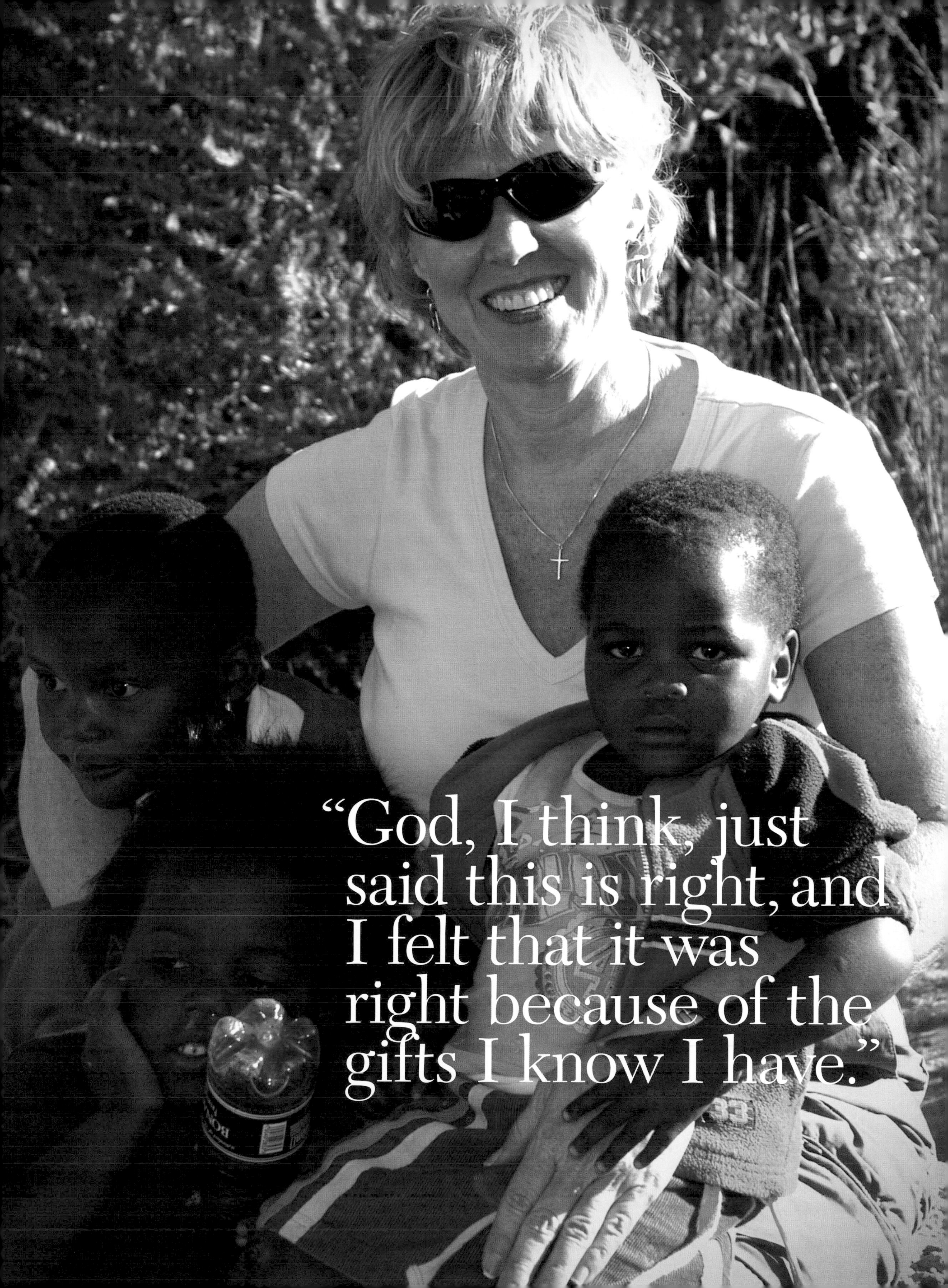
"God, I think, just
said this is right, and
I felt that it was
right because of the
gifts I know I have."

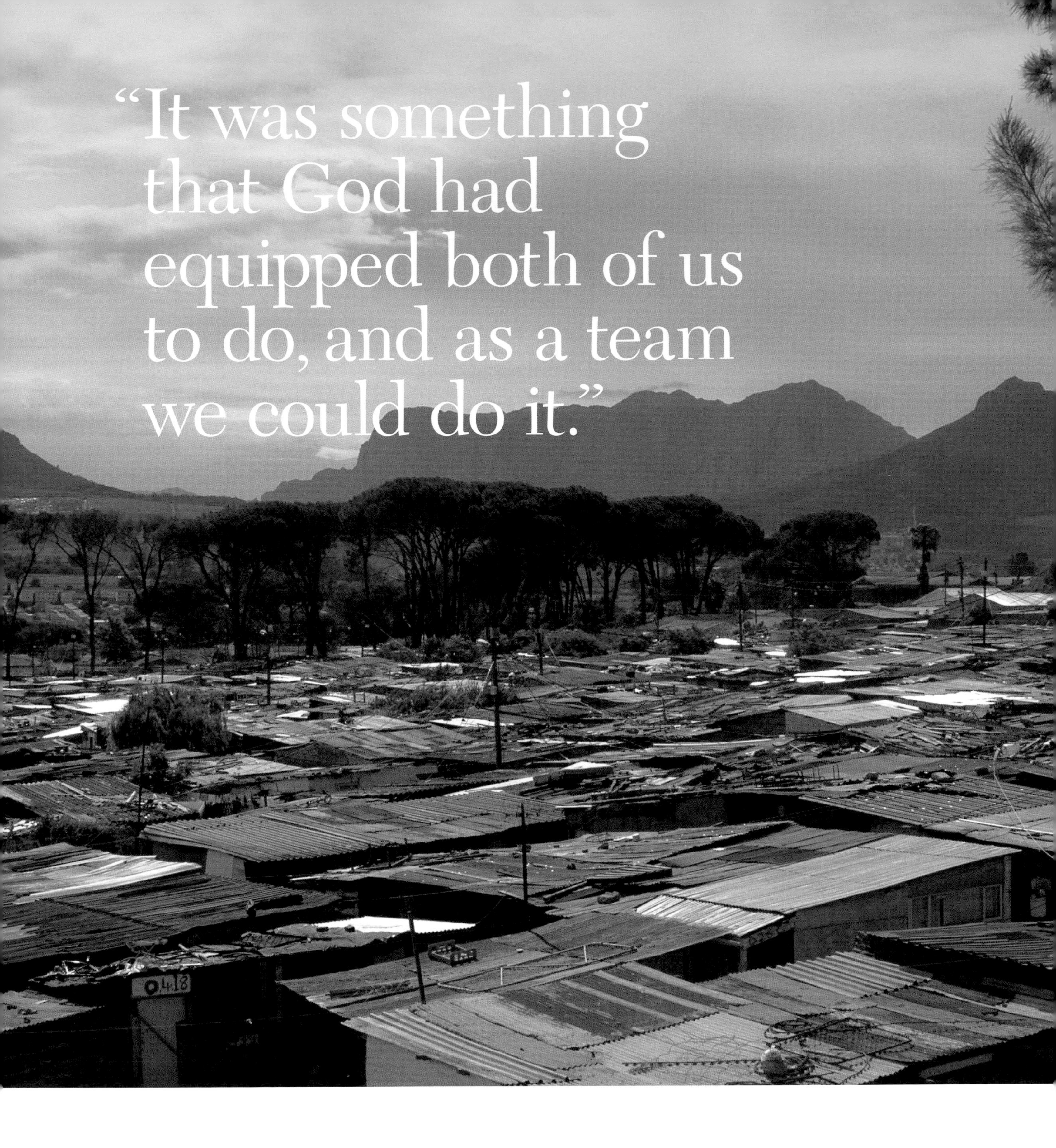

> "It was something that God had equipped both of us to do, and as a team we could do it."

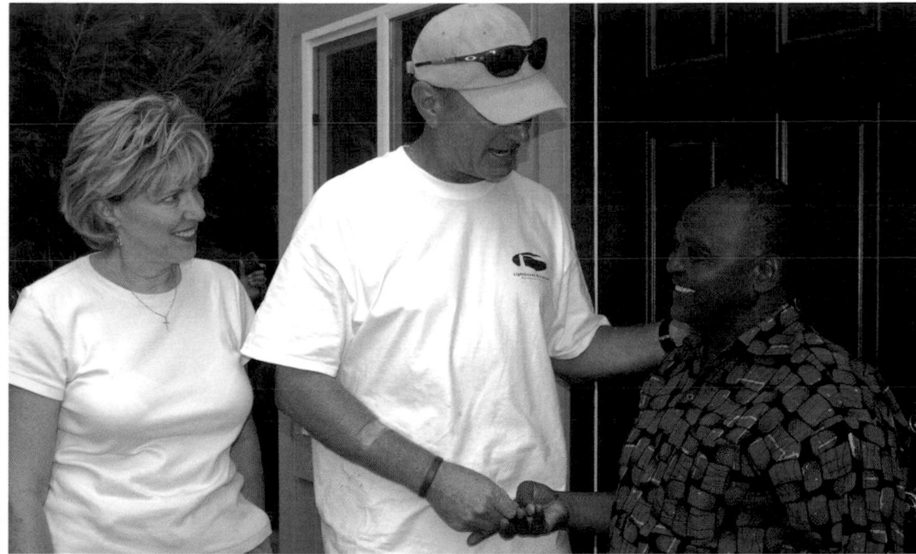

are you going to do it? If you wait five years or you wait 10 years until you've got everything that you want financially, it's a fool's game because at that point your Halftime moment has passed you by."

HopeBuilders began as a way to mobilize people and resources from their church to help individuals and families who are living in deteriorated housing. In an effort that pre-dates but is similar to the TV show *Extreme Makeover: Home Edition*, HopeBuilders brings in a volunteer team of carpenters, plumbers, electricians and painters for a quick-turn remodeling effort. "We use it as an opportunity to be the hands and feet of Jesus," Cliff explains, "to share God's love with these people."

Their second initiative, Tapestry Homes, addresses inadequate housing in the slums of foreign countries. In squatter communities around the world, families live in one-room homes with mud floors and walls pieced together with scraps of wood, plastic, corrugated metal and street signs. The fire-prone shanty houses stand inches from each other in places like Kayamandi, South Africa, where 30,000 people live within a one-square-mile area outside of Cape Town.

Tapestry's original plan called for buying land near squatter communities, building pre-manufactured homes and moving families.

"We quickly learned that in the midst of this chaotic life experience … there is tremendous community and interdependence," Cliff says. "You might have a family here and the mother, if she is still living, because unfortunately most people are

"It gives you more energy to go on. For me, it gives me faith, affirmation, and confirmation that we're doing the right thing, that we're going down the right path."

dying of AIDS, needs to run an errand or go to work, and so her children need to be taken care of by her neighbor while she is away. To take people out of their community would be wrong."

The availability and cost of land also made relocation plans difficult, so Tapestry Homes switched to a "shack replacement" strategy. In one day, they can take out an existing shack and replace it with a home that is elevated off the ground and has insulated, fire-resistant panels for walls.

"That's what distinguishes Tapestry Homes from other housing relief organizations," Cliff says. "We're not pulling them out of the community, and we're much more than just relief housing. We're building housing that will endure for a number of years, but make an eternal difference."

The organization eventually wants to start an in-country manufacturing plant that will provide jobs while building the components of the homes. As the vision expands, of course, so do the challenges. But those faith-stretching challenges make the rewards of helping others all the sweeter.

"It gives you more energy to go on," Rose says. "For me, it strengthens my faith and confirms that we're doing the right thing, that we're going down the right path. While there are hiccups along the way, this is the path we're supposed to be on because it's those little signs that say, 'Keep going, keep going. You're going to help another person. Keep going.' " HT

For additional information and helpful Web links related to Cliff and Rose's journey from success to significance, visit www.halftime.org/thesecondhalf and click on their names.

2006 Yale
Christian
Business
Conference
FAITH & ETHICS
IN THE
WORKPLACE

STUART HALL

Connecting the dots

DAVID MILLER

The next generation of leaders wrestles almost daily in colleges with the toughest issues facing our culture. For me, college was only about preparing for a life of business, not a place I ever considered revisiting.

Yet a growing number of our peers are wondering how they can invest their life experiences from within ivy-covered buildings.

They end up impacting the lives of thousands of students – students such as the son of a friend of mine who was attending Yale when he met David Miller, then a professor and the executive director of the Yale Center for Faith and Culture. My friend's son, a smart student and a talented golfer with a great heart and solid character, sought out David as a mentor, and David's investment in this young man's life was priceless.

David was just helping him connect the dots in life. After all, David's spent much of his own life connecting dots, and his second-half career has become an extension of that process.

"My personal mission statement is to help leaders, current or future, integrate the claims of their faith with the demands of their work," David says. "That's what I do. I do it through teaching in and outside the classroom. I do it through my research and writing, and ... I also do a lot of advisory and consulting work."

David, who now is director of the Princeton University Faith and Work Initiative, sees teaching as the perfect second-half platform. He has Ivy League credibility, an opportunity to influence some of the country's brightest future leaders and, through the Avodah Institute he co-founded in 1999, the freedom to work with business leaders who are living out the theology he studies and teaches.

Like so many people featured in this book, David never expected to end up where he is. He got there only by hearing God's call, moving him from being an investment banker to professor. His quest, however, was and is to connect the dots between Sunday and Monday.

You see, David started out as the same sort of intellectually gifted student that he often sees in his classroom, and he had hard questions about his faith. His mother held fast to what he respectfully saw as a "simple" and unquestioning faith, while his father, a "genius" and a scientist, struggled to believe in anything he couldn't fully intellectually comprehend.

David, whose early career took him on IBM's fast track and then, at age 29, to the London office of States Street Bank & Trust as managing director of the bank's European operations, wrestled with understanding the relationship between his deep faith and life in the marketplace. While he was in England, David and his wife, Karen, ended up in a small fellowship group led by the renowned pastor and theologian John Stott, who helped David see that it's "theologically sound to have hard tough questions."

"If God is really who God says He is, and if Christ is really who He said He is, I don't need to be afraid of the hard questions," David says. "In fact, I should embrace them and run with them."

David embraces them and encourages his students to do so, as well, something he says greatly appeals to them because so many have never been given intellectual permission to do so. Many of them, in fact, are steered well clear of integrating their faith with their academic or professional lives.

Stott also helped feed David's curiosity about the theology of work. Stott teaches "the ultimate centrality of Jesus," David says, and that means, "if you accept the proposition of who Jesus said He was then your life is irrevocably changed and how you live your life matters. In all walks of life, whether you are an investment banker, a ditch digger, a CEO, or a secretary, your faith matters."

This was freeing for David, because it allowed him to see his work in banking as his ministry and his calling. And that's why his return to academia seemed so out of the blue. David and Karen were in a sweet spot in life. He loved his career in banking. And Karen, who earned degrees

"Resoundingly, they all say trying to live out their faith was the smartest thing they ever did. They usually will say it was the times when they didn't or when they compromised that ended up being the mistakes."

from Lehigh, Georgetown and Harvard Law, had established herself as a bright legal mind, both as a practitioner and as a professor.

"We were at a stage of life where we couldn't have been happier, quite frankly," David says. "Karen and I were both professionally satisfied." Then came an unexplainable "tugging" at his heart. "Why would God take me out of that very zone that I thrived in and enjoyed?" David wondered.

It took about 18 months, but with the help of Karen and other friends, David confirmed this wasn't some "mid-life wanderlust." So he and Karen returned to the United States. He earned a master's degree in divinity and a Ph.D. in ethics, both at Princeton Theological Seminary and all with a burning question at the heart of his studies: What did Jesus, the Bible and all the great thinkers in church history have to say about life in the marketplace?

As it turned out, plenty, and that's what David teaches to students, business leaders and anyone else who's interested, both through his work as a professor and through the Avodah Institute.

Today he's helping leaders find the freedom to integrate their faith into their everyday decisions by using language that's winsome, persuasive and attractive. "You live a healthier, more successful career and life if you put your faith first and then figure out how to connect the dots," he says. "But the question from students is, 'Does it work? If I do this am I just setting myself up to be a wimp, and a pushover? Am I going to be able to get ahead in a business that rewards cutthroat behavior?' "

To help allay the question of utility, David usually invites CEOs who take their faith seriously to talk frankly to students about the decisions they've made – the good and bad ones – and what role their faith played. "As they look back over the arc of a multi-decade career," David says, "what's the report card? Resoundingly, they all say trying to live out their faith was the smartest thing they ever did. They usually will say it was the times when they didn't or when they compromised that ended up being the mistakes."

David is careful not to promote a view that integrating one's faith in the workplace automatically leads to success, but he wants his students to see the benefits – sometimes internal and, yes, sometimes financial – to integrating one's faith in one's work.

The hardest place, however, to live out one's faith sometimes is much more personal. In fact, one of his toughest challenges was when Karen's career as an attorney and law professor was cut short more than a decade ago after she was diagnosed with Multiple Sclerosis. She and David had to wrestle with all the complex questions that came with that change in their lives and, as David puts it, "I'd be kidding if I said it was a smooth, linear process."

"Karen getting MS is not a blessing," he says, "it's a horrible thing, and I sure wish she didn't have it. I'd do anything to take it myself so she didn't have to have it, so I wouldn't call it a blessing. What I would say, profoundly, is that we've felt the love and presence of God more deeply in our marriage."

Karen is finding new ways to direct her heart and intellect, while also working full-time at the job of resisting the progression of her disease. They have learned that callings take many shapes, and God is present through them all, helping to connect the dots and fulfill His purpose through our lives. HT

For additional information and helpful Web links related to David's journey from success to significance, visit www.halftime.org/thesecondhalf and click on his name.

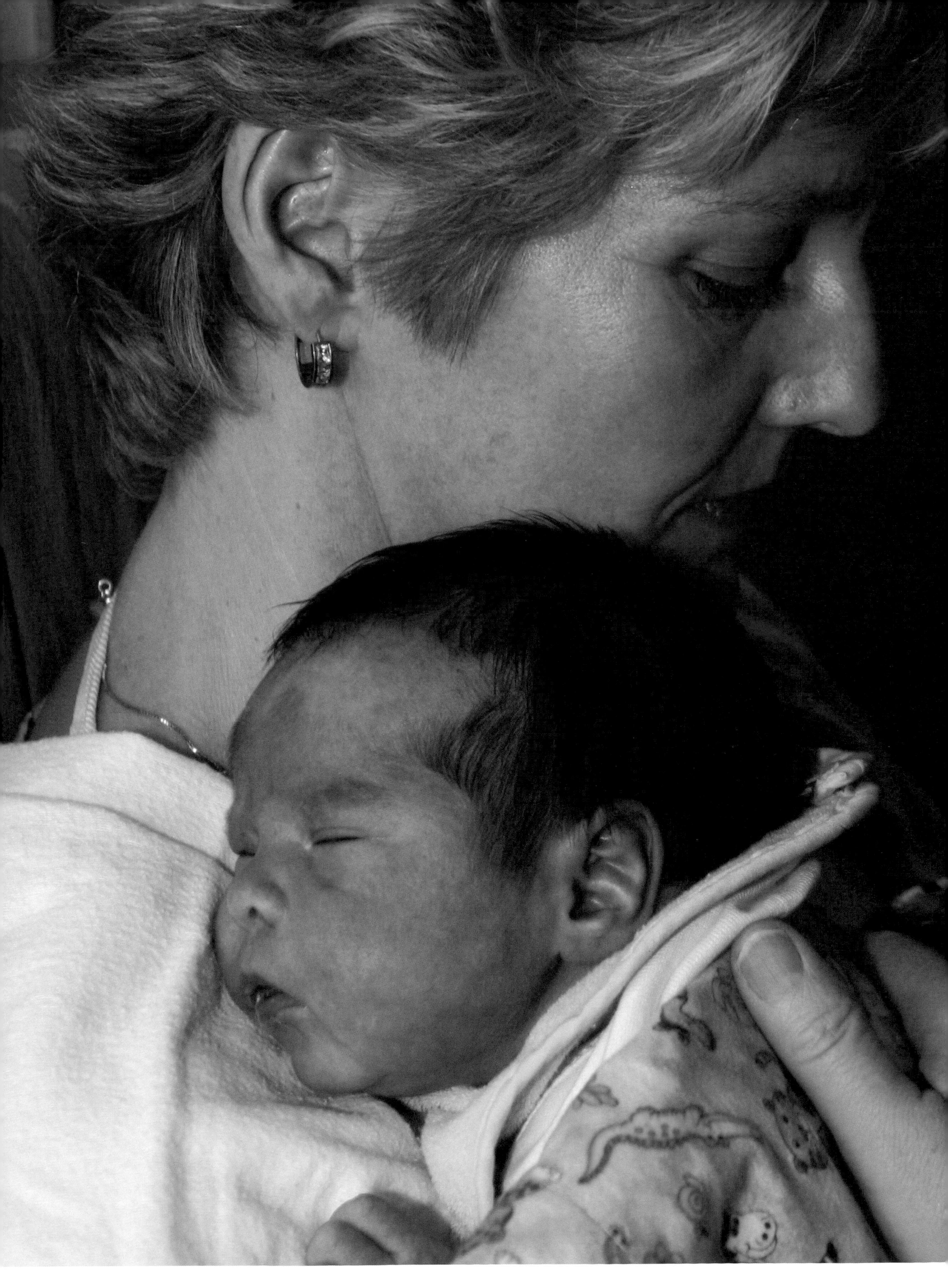

Rocking the world

SANDY GRIFFITH

You can see it in the pictures, can't you? Sandy Griffith has an overwhelming love for these babies. But to be really frank, I find her faith somewhat unnerving.

We'd known each other for, I don't know, maybe three years when I called Sandy to chat. She was surrounded by real storms in her life. Her sister was at her parent's home recuperating from brain surgery when her father learned he'd need surgery on his spinal cord. And the stress of it all led to a full-blown flare up of her mother's arthritis. "She's on a cane, my dad's on a walker, my sister's on the couch, and I'm shuttle bussing here, there and everywhere," Sandy said at the time. "Life's just a little upside down."

If there's one thing I've seen in Sandy, it's the ability to find peace in life's storms – in part by her practice of bringing peace into the life storms of others. A week or two before our conversation, for instance, on a rainy Friday morning when she could have stayed home from both the storms of nature and the storms of life, Sandy took on the rain and the traffic and drove into one of the toughest sections of downtown Houston to Ben Taub General Hospital. Then she made her way to the high-risk nursery

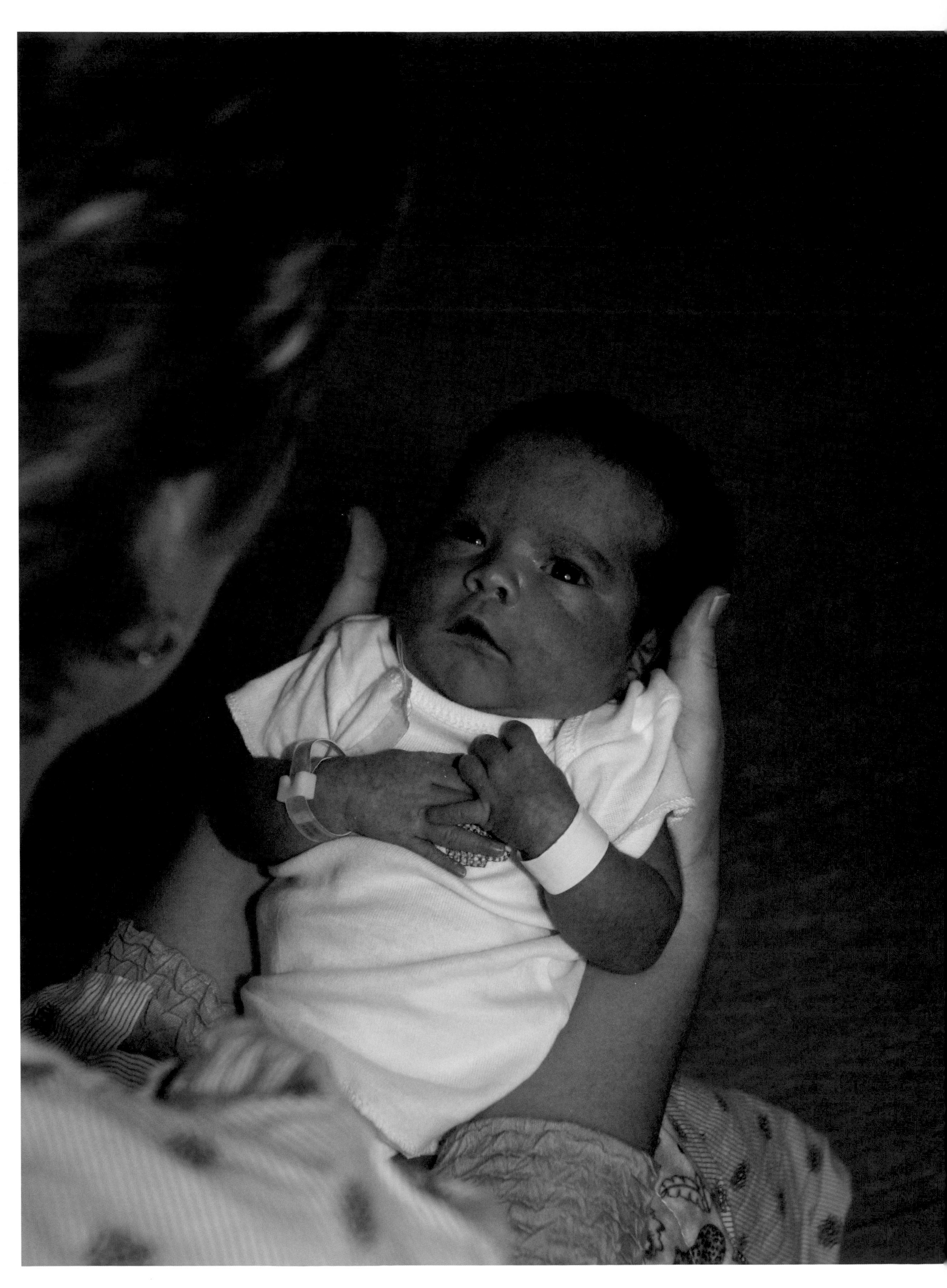

"If He really is who we believe He is, there's no end to the hope that God's got it well in hand. If you look at the statistics and go read your *Newsweek*, chances are this baby has no life ahead of him. I just choose not to believe that."

unit, settled into a rocking chair with the baby of a heroine addict and counted her family's blessings. It's her calling but also her therapy. Unlike most of our peers at midlife, Sandy knows without any doubt that she has discovered her place of greatest calling for the second half of her life – right there in the rocking chair with the baby of a drug addict.

"This little baby had just been taken off the Methadone ... and he was suffering horribly," she says. "As long as you were holding him he was happy, but if you put him down, even to change his diaper, he screamed.

"I just pulled up a chair, picked him up and held him for about three hours. He slept peacefully in my arms, and it was an amazing moment because his ability to rest in my arms was such a picture of my ability to rest while holding him. It was like both of us were being fed, because all I wanted in the world was a peaceful place. ... So I'm sitting there holding this little guy, knowing that this is the only real peace that he's going to have that day because there isn't anybody else to hold him."

Years earlier, Sandy was rocking her own premature baby when she realized this was her area of passion. As she sat and rocked her son, she noticed there was no one to hold and love most of the other babies in the NICU. Their mothers had been discharged, and most had returned to work. The nurses could feed them and change them but did not have time to hold them.

Once her own kids had grown, Sandy realized that "raising kids was fun and significant, but they don't need me like they used to. So who am I going to be now that I am all grown up?"

As she explored opportunities with preemie babies, almost every door closed on her until she and a friend arrived at

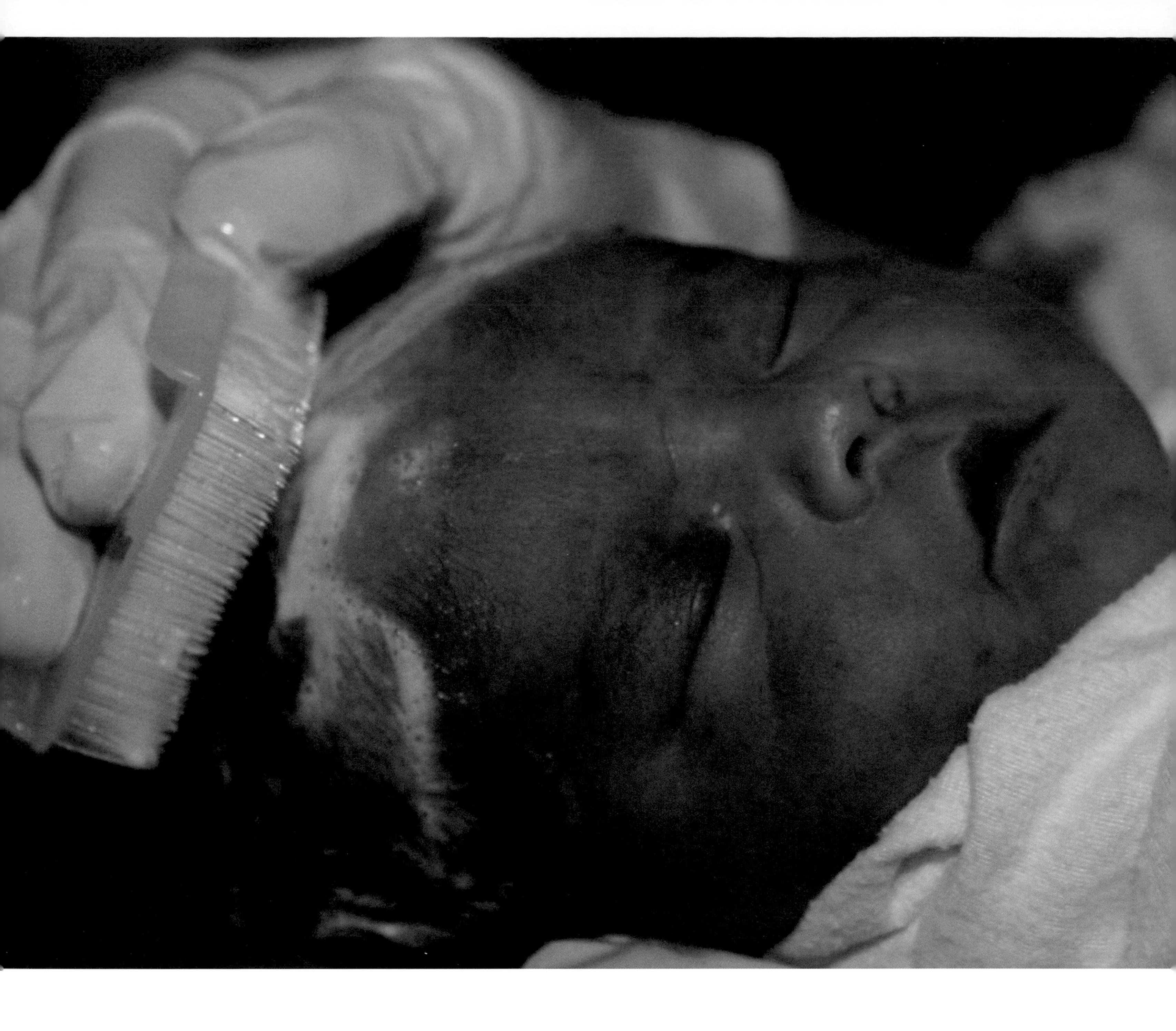

Ben Taub's high-risk unit. She quickly realized that these were the babies who really needed what she had to offer. These were the abandoned babies, often the children of young drug addicts who come in, have their babies and then disappear.

"Looking back on it, I can see that God had been working on me the whole time," Sandy says. "But until I went to the place where He wanted me to go, He wasn't just going to let me get safe and comfortable in an environment that didn't need me."

Sandy goes to Ben Taub Hospital almost every Friday to rock the babies, feed the babies, pray for the babies and hopefully intersect in the lives of those young moms. Along the way, she's prepared the path for other women to do the same. She's organized donations of rocking chairs, furniture and other wish-list items for the unit. In fact, her work helped the hospital build an apartment suite inside the unit so that those young moms don't have to vanish in the middle of the night. They can live with, and learn to care for, their babies while still under the supervision of the nurses. She and her friends are providing an alternative, some encouragement and support to moms in one of Houston's most impoverished areas.

A decade ago, she would have become jaded and depressed working in such circumstances, but she's developed a faith that God's at work even in the most horrific of situations. "There is hope in everything," she says. "If He really is who I believe He is, there's no end to the hope that God's got it well in hand. If you look at the statistics and go read your *Newsweek*, chances are this baby has no life ahead of him. I just choose not to believe that."

See, this is the faith I see in Sandy that I find unnerving.

Sandy regularly prays that God will pull the babies out of their bad circumstances and provide for them in ways that no one can foresee. She sees hope in the

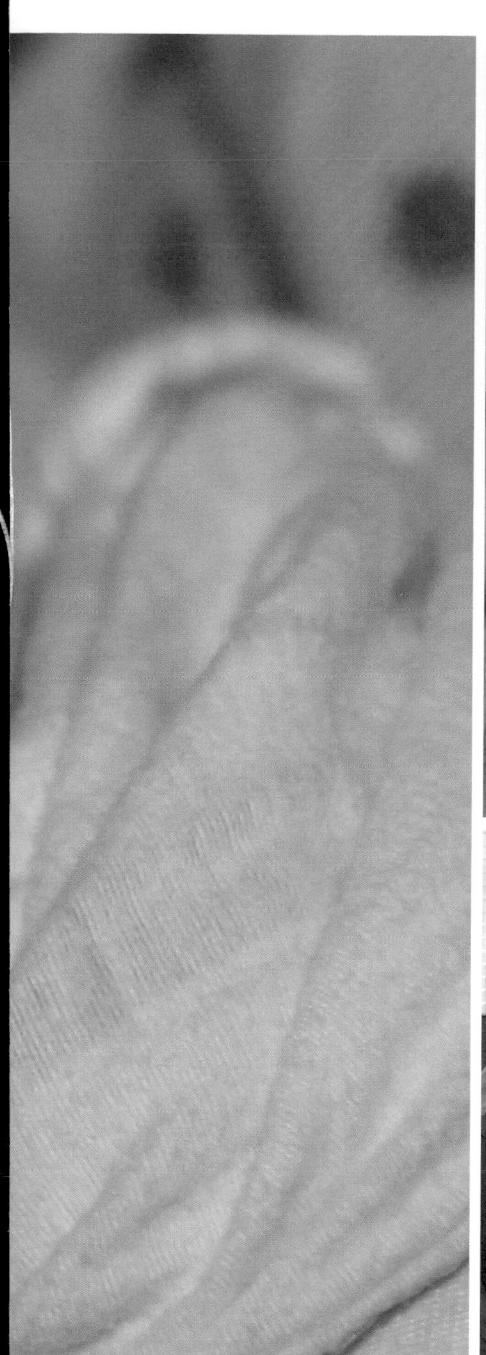

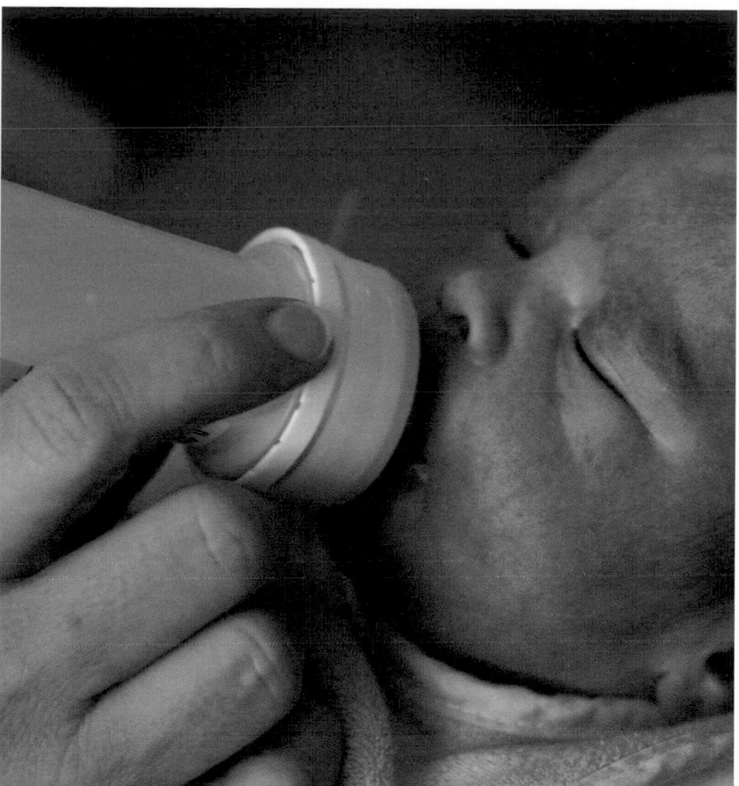

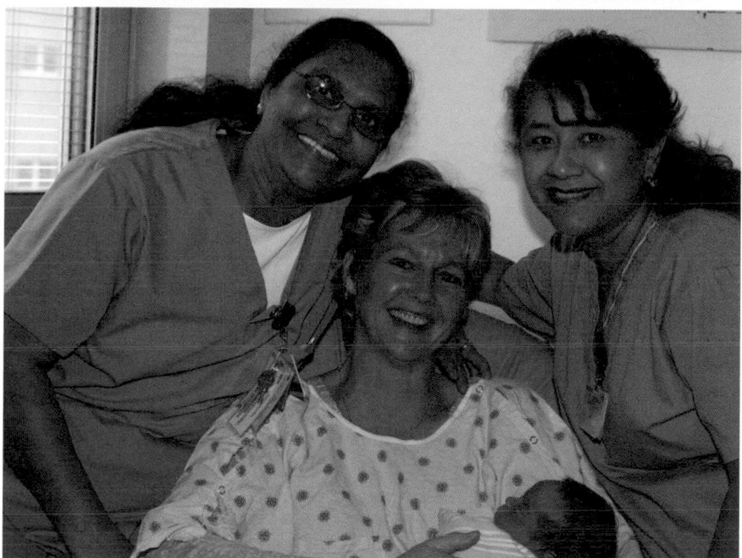

hopelessness. "I've seen it happen and I know it could, so I'm just going to pray that it will and know that He's in charge," she says. "As long as I'm where He asked me to be, and I'm praying the prayers, He's going to honor that. I just have a confidence about it."

As Sandy's rocking chair ministry drew attention outside her circle of friends and family, she and her husband David, a successful attorney, began seeing the greater significance of her obedience. "In the beginning, it was 'another one of those little projects that Sandy has,'" Sandy reflects. "I think David's come to realize that beyond the shadow of a doubt this is God's calling, and I'm doing something important. Both of us have been on that road of learning. All I do is rock babies. It's totally feeding me, and it's so easy to do."

Too often, Sandy says, people do nothing because they believe what they have to offer simply isn't good enough. In doing that, they might miss out.

"I had to be available and obedient," she says. "I didn't have to have a million dollars." HT

For additional information and helpful Web links related to Sandy's journey from success to significance, visit www.halftime.org/thesecondhalf and click on her name.

Surrender yourself

BOB AND TINA MUZIKOWSKI

Bob Muzikowski is a modern-day prophet. So while I love hanging out with him, I seldom come away feeling comfortable. He lives compassion with abandon. His life challenges me to the core.

"The doorbell rings," Bob will tell you, "and a problem comes."

Problems? Challenges? Crisis? Stress? Call them what you will, but there's no avoiding them for Bob and his family, not since they committed to "doing" something about life in inner-city Chicago.

It's 10:30 p.m. and the boy ringing the doorbell this time is 11 years old. He's been locked out of his house and has nowhere to go. Bob suspects the boy's mother is high again, so he doesn't take him home. He offers him a sandwich and lets him sleep on the couch. "I just think that's what the Bible says to do," Bob explains. "Don't tell them to come back tomorrow if you have it with you today."

Bob might end up as the best man at this boy's wedding or at his college graduation or with him on the day he signs the loan for his first home. Since moving to the inner city and starting what's grown into the largest inner-city Little League baseball

CHICAGO HOPE
ACADEMY

program in the country in the mid-1990s, Bob often experiences the joys that come with changed lives. He's seen addicts clean up and get jobs. He's "given away" young women at their weddings, knowing that something as simple as baseball helped them avoid a life of prostitution. And through a new high school he helped launch, he's beginning to see even more rewarding stories.

But he also knows the boy ringing his doorbell soon might end up like so many others from his neighborhood – on the streets, in jail or dead. Bob's given generously to kids who have turned around and stolen from him. He's helped boys and girls enroll in the new school, only to see them get kicked out because of behavioral issues. And, perhaps most painfully, he recalls the boy who came to baseball practice on a bike with tireless rims. For the boy's birthday, Bob and a friend fixed up the bike. A few weeks later, someone shot the child – for his bike. "We're not going to win all of these battles," he says softly.

Until recently, Bob still worked several days a week as a benefits planner for a large insurance company, spending much of his professional life in a high-rise Chicago office building. Today his office is on the other side of town in Chicago's "Near West" area, which also is where he lives with his wife Tina and their seven children.

The picture of inner-city Chicago has changed for the better thanks to Bob and Tina. Bob started the neighborhood Little League program as a way to bring children and adults of different backgrounds together for friendly competition. (His 2001 book *Safe at Home* chronicles this story.) The program now operates in two areas of Chicago, as well as in New York City.

"I just wanted to do something, having no idea it would grow up into being a giant part of our life," he says. "And maybe a too giant part of our life now."

He and Tina also founded Chicago Hope Academy, turning an abandoned Catholic elementary school in their neighborhood into a private high school that offers a faith-based education to inner-city students. He serves as the school's president. More than the $1 million plus they have already invested of their own money in these kids, they bring a vision and passion that has helped the school recruit top-tier teachers. One teacher I had lunch with was a bright young man right out of Yale. When I asked him why he chose to work here, he said because it's a chance to make a real difference in these kids' lives.

Bob provides operational leadership, raises money for the school and brings to each kid a firm handshake and a look in the eyes that says, "I believe in you." Not only was I deeply moved by his intense compassion for the kids, but also by his audacity to build a culture that enables Chicago Hope Academy to be the only high school in the state of Illinois where there are no locks on the lockers. Go figure.

His greatest quests, however, always include getting people personally involved. He often points to the words of Isaiah,

"I just wanted to do something, having no idea it would grow up into being a giant part of our life."

75
98
8
53
87
29

…spending yourself on others means seeing a need and meeting that need. It means writing a check, but it also might mean coaching third base.

who, quoting God, writes that "if you spend yourselves in behalf of the hungry and satisfy the needs of the oppressed, then your light will rise in the darkness, and your night will become like the noonday." To Bob the phrase "spend yourselves" is key, because it indicates personal involvement, not just going to a "black-tie affair for the homeless and throwing a thousand dollars on the plate."

"It's got to cost you," he says. "And it has cost us."

Time spent on the baseball program and school often was time away from developing new clients and more business. "We've made half of what we would make, which is still too much anyway," he says. Bob and his family set the bar high for the rest of us – by living on a tenth of his income and giving away the rest.

You and I may find that hard to swallow right off – but give it some more careful thought. When I visit Bob and hang out with the students he is impacting I begin to understand how saving the life of one of these kids makes you think differently about how you spend on yourself.

As I reflect on Bob and Tina's life, it's not so much about what they gave up as what they got by trading up. When they opted to invest in kids' lives instead of themselves, they traded up for rewards they sometimes see immediately but other times are years in the making.

If you stop by the Chicago Hope Academy to see for yourself (and I strongly encourage you to do so), Bob will tell you that spending yourself on others means seeing a need and meeting that need. It means writing a check, but it also might mean coaching third base. And it might mean downsizing to a smaller home, quitting the expensive country club, driving a modestly priced car or living in the inner city.

"I think it's just that we're supposed to be obedient," to the call on our second half, he says. "As simple as that … we're just supposed to be obedient and do it." HT

For additional information and helpful Web links related to Bob's journey from success to significance, visit www.halftime.org/thesecondhalf and click on his name.

The sum of it all

JEFF STEDMAN

Jeff Stedman might look like an analytical chief financial officer, but he feels deeply the pain of kids who are having a tough time growing up. His eyes fill with tears and his voice breaks when he talks about the privilege he now has of helping kids in trouble.

What drives that passion? I wondered as Jeff and I visited early one morning in the dining room of the Broadmoor Hotel, just a short stroll away from his home in Colorado Springs, Colo.

Turns out, Jeff had a tough childhood himself. His parents divorced. His mother was an alcoholic and drug addict. They spent a lot of time "moving around, getting evicted." And he

"went to seven different schools the first four years of elementary school." As a result, he was just drifting, looking for some place to belong.

"In high school I played baseball, but I got cut because I was out drinking on weekends and wasn't practicing," he says. "While I did have a passion for it, I didn't have a direction or any goals about it. Then, God sent me an angel."

In his senior year of high school, Jeff had a locker next to the "prettiest girl" in school. "It was amazing," he says. "One day she offered me a Tootsie Roll lollipop … and I took that and parlayed it into some conversations, and I spent a lot more time around my locker waiting for her to show up. We became friends and later started dating and she became something that was, for the first time in my life, far greater than I ever thought I could achieve.

"She asked, or demanded, a few things that I needed to change in my life, including hanging out with some of the folks I hung out with and doing some of the things I did, and so my life started changing. I quickly went from an underachiever to … an over-achiever. When I got into college I got out three-and-a-half years later with a double major in accounting and finance."

Jeff's job with a public accounting firm opened the doors for him to work with entrepreneur Lee Roy Mitchell, who put Jeff's energy, passion and analytical skills to work for Cinemark Theaters. At age 30, Jeff became the company's chief financial officer.

In the 1990s, Cinemark grew almost tenfold to a company with more than $800 million in revenues and 3,000 screens. Jeff, who helped raise more than $1 billion in capital during those years, credits Lee Roy with giving him the opportunities to pick up "a lot of creative skill sets – the ability to pass on a vision and tell a story and to follow through and execute on that story. It was an incredible journey."

Oh yeah, and along the way he married Lisa – the "prettiest girl" from high school, whose locker had been next to his.

As he clicked through the milestones

of success, however, Jeff felt a "sense of loss and emptiness" in his life. Then in 1997, at Lee Roy's invitation, Jeff and Lisa went to a Young Life camp so they could learn more about the organization Cinemark supported financially. When they got to the camp, they were immediately struck by the sense of God's love and compassion for the kids. Lisa had been a Christian since junior high, but Jeff didn't begin a relationship with God until that weekend at the Young Life camp. He was 34 years old.

Lisa was "blown away," he says, but also scared by where such a radical change in Jeff's heart might take them. As it turned out, it took them to the Rocky Mountains, but only after Jeff and Lisa caught a vision for how his skills and experience in the world of finance could help meet the needs of millions of kids who are adrift like he was growing up.

Jeff will tell you that his background has given him "an incredible amount of empathy for people that live in tragic situations and have dysfunctional families. You know, the kids that are lost but … may not know that God is going to be pursuing, protecting them and sending angels all along."

Now, as you may know, the theater business is all about "butts in seats." The more seats that are full, the more money you make. Below the surface of that simple formula, however, there are complex financial systems that help make it work efficiently and profitably. Imagine taking the skills of the CFO of a large theater chain and using them to help a global organization change teens' lives forever rather than just entertain folks for 90 minutes.

Jeff didn't jump at Young Life's offer to join their team. He loved what Young Life does for high school kids who are at a precarious stage in their lives. However, it seemed ridiculous to consider leaving the life he and Lisa enjoyed. His latest business venture was turning into a financial success. Plus, they had settled into their lives in Austin, Texas. It was home. It was where they wanted to raise their budding family.

"It was probably the happiest we'd

"It was probably the happiest we'd ever been in our adult lives."

ever been in our adult lives," he says.

Increasingly, it became clear to Jeff that God had prepared him not only professionally for the role at Young Life, but emotionally and spiritually, as well. "God walked me through the first 43 years of my life specifically for this," he says. "Lisa got to that same conclusion. I didn't see how we could not do this. It was clear. We were supposed to be there."

When Jeff arrived at Young Life as CFO, he realized just how helpful his skills and experiences would be. Within two years, he had replaced many antiquated financial systems enabling the organization to pass approximately $1 million in savings on to its field ministries while adding greater accountability. Most of all, Jeff loves the thousands of hours it saved Young Life staff that they can now spend with kids. He also helped redesign the model for funding camps scholarships, all with an eye toward getting more students involved. Now he'd come full circle, back to "butts in seats."

Jeff knows that every empty place at a camp each summer is a lost opportunity to change a kid's life, and seeing the changed lives in kids is what drives his passion and fuels his gratitude.

"God allowed us to participate in all this stuff," Jeff says. "He doesn't *need* us to participate in any of this stuff. He *allows* us to do it only because He wants us to know how deeply He loves us. We are feeling that, so it's an exciting way to live life. It's an abundant life." HT

For additional information and helpful Web links related to Jeff's journey from success to significance, visit www.halftime.org/thesecondhalf and click on his name.

Ambassador of compassion

LEO ABDELLA

My guess is that Leo Abdella and I like hanging out together and understand each other so well because we are both "recovering real estate developers." See, it just gets into your blood.

Even when you feel called in a different direction for your second half, it's still in there. We drive around West Palm Beach, Fla., together looking at cranes, and architecture design and properties. In fact, Leo moved here intent on resurrecting his career as a developer, and, in retrospect, that's exactly what he did. He just never imagined he'd be developing service opportunities rather than beach condos and retirement villas.

"The real estate industry – and the development side of the real estate industry – is an interesting education process of how so many moving parts fit to make this engine work," Leo says. "I use that experience every day in my current life."

Leo, the missions and outreach pastor for Christ Fellowship in Palm Beach Gardens, Fla., began his professional career in real

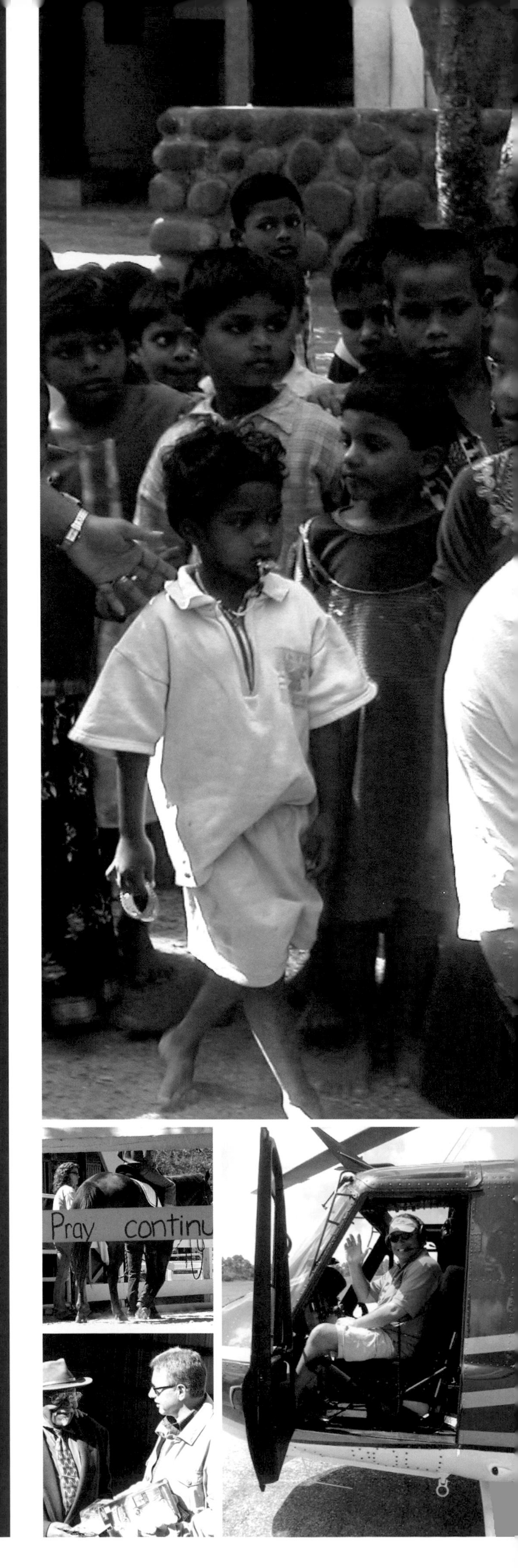

estate and quickly became a junior partner in a firm that specialized in second homes around the ski areas and lakes of New Hampshire. "We did everything from buy the land, develop the land, do all of the site work on the land, do the architecture, build the buildings, and furnish the buildings," Leo says.

The company did well until 1987 when the stock market crashed, causing a landslide of real estate values and property foreclosures. "Virtually overnight I went from making millions building high-end resort homes to losing millions to owing millions," says Leo. "It was brutal. ... Before the crash, I lived in the work-hard, play-hard world of materialism. I thought that it was all under my control – that I could earn every thing, do anything. Then it was all gone."

After a dissatisfying stretch managing foreclosed properties for banks, he and his family moved to south Florida. "We really thought that we would get into the same business down here," he says, "but it didn't work out that way, not at all."

Instead, Leo and his wife Candace followed their teenage daughter to a church, where they began to explore spiritual things and launched into a new kind of relationship with God. With that new perspective, they began looking for ways to focus the second half of life on helping others rather than helping their bank account. In particular, Leo felt drawn toward global relief work.

"It became clear to me that God had prepared me to be a facilitator for those who can't do it on their own, an ambassador of compassion," Leo said.

Leo, who came by his work ethic from his depression-era parents, began putting his experiences as a facilitator of development deals to work with a friend who had been a missionary in South America. They started a company that imported and exported a natural nutritional product, then used its profits to fund missionaries, children's homes and schools in the jungles of Peru. Six years later, Leo pursued his second-half calling as an ambassador of compassion and founded MedCorps International Foundation. He used his contacts in the natural products industry to make deals for nutritional products that, for one reason or another, were no longer of use to the companies. He then shipped them to partner organizations serving the needy all around the world. Leo says, "A little nutrition can make a huge difference in millions of peoples lives."

In one case, a company bought out a competitor and decided to discontinue a

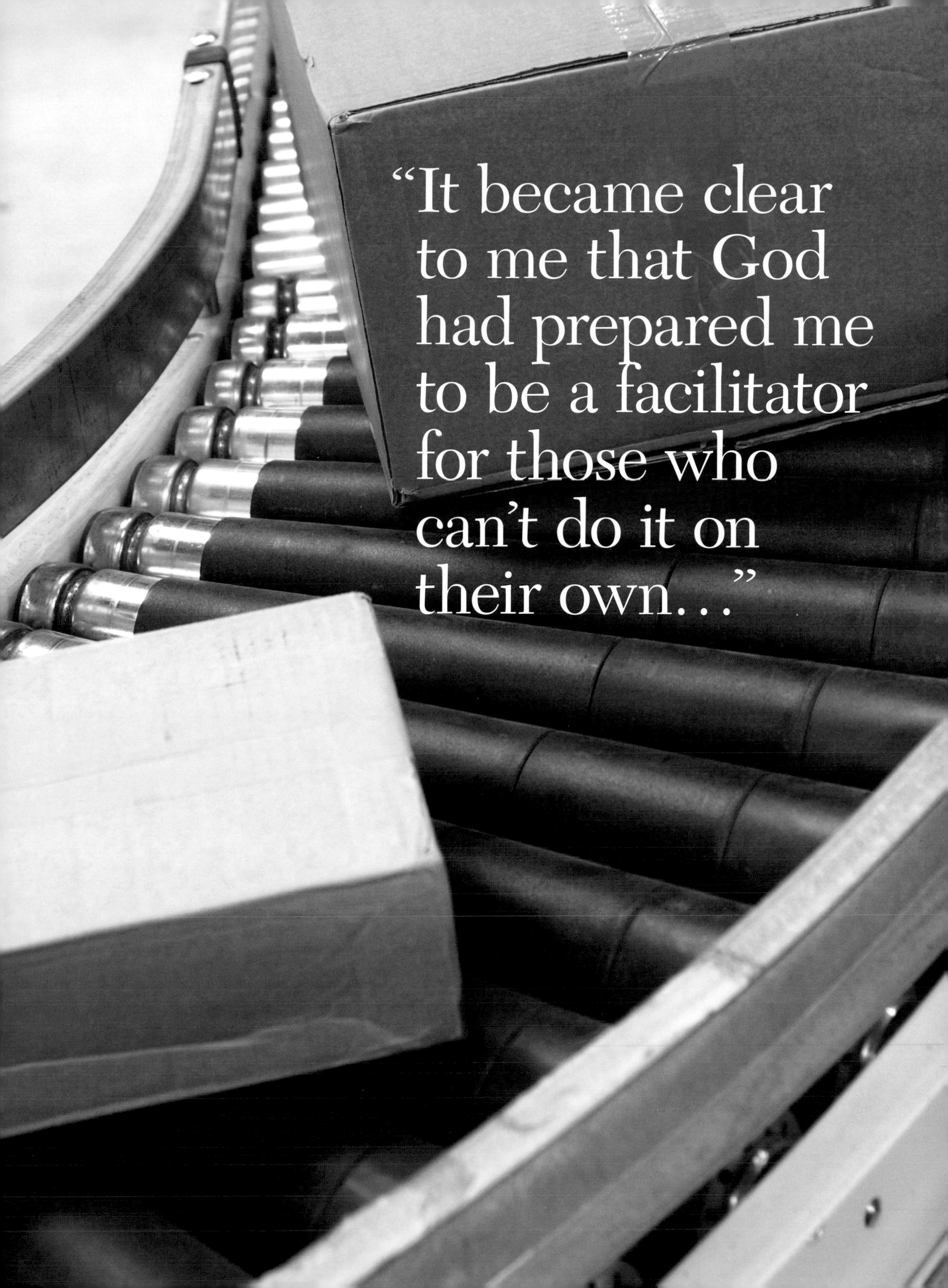
"It became clear
to me that God
had prepared me
to be a facilitator
for those who
can't do it on
their own…"

product line designed to help enhance children's neurological development. The supplements came in what looked and tasted like candy bars and shakes, and the company asked Leo to take them off its hands.

"They faxed me a list, and it was five 40-foot trailer loads full of this stuff," he says. "We're going to bless the socks off the kids all over the world. Sure enough, that's what we did."

Leo continued to connect resources with missionary organizations that focused on serving the poor, which made him a natural fit when Tom Mullins, his pastor at Christ Fellowship, recruited him to lead the mega church's missions and outreach department.

Leo not only energized the missions' efforts, but also looked for creative ways to connect its members to all sorts of projects, local and international, ranging from inner-city, to the migrant worker, to health care advocacy for single moms, to children's homes and medical supply delivery. Leo started with 900 square feet of space to create a "clubhouse" where he invites business leaders for brainstorming sessions to help solve a range of community social problems.

Seven years later, the space has grown into 3,000 square feet called The Outreach Center, and the number of marketplace leaders has grown, as well as the scope of the projects they take on. Leo believes that the intersection of compassion and commerce creates a unique place for talented marketplace leaders to fulfill the second half of their lives.

Leo sees his work focusing more and

Those whose hearts love horses and have a passion to serve special-needs kids could not find more pleasure – just to hear the giggle of a little girl who for a few moments is lost in a new world with a wonderful, gentle animal.

more on helping plug business leaders into projects that fit their skills and experiences. And in a church with more than 15,000 people many Sundays, there are lots of them.

"Our churches are filled with people from the marketplace who come with life skills multiple times more interesting than mine," he says. "It's only a matter of us figuring out how we harness that, motivate that, encourage that, and empower them. The possibilities of what can be done just thrill me. Their skills, compassion and creativity can impact generations. … That fires me up."

So let me take you to a place where compassion and commerce converge. It's early on a Saturday morning, and trailers begin backing up to one side of a small parcel of land purchased by business individuals. They're unloading horses from some of the wealthiest polo communities around and putting them in the newly constructed open stalls. On the other side of the riding ring, families pull up in minivans so that their disabled children can enjoy the therapeutic value of riding one of these well-trained horses. Those whose hearts love horses and have a passion to serve special-needs kids could not find more pleasure – just to hear the giggle of a little girl who for a few moments is lost in a new world with a wonderful, gentle animal. And in my book, God smiles at that.

It's simple but transformational for everyone involved. Now that fires me up. HT

For additional information and helpful Web links related to Leo's journey from success to significance, visit www.halftime.org/thesecondhalf and click on his name.

MERCY

Mercy

Finding life's pizzazz

LINDA HOOD

Linda Hood and I sat down to chat in a noisy, crowded coffee shop – not the ideal place for me to ask Linda's advice about something one of our teenage girls was wrestling with.

In a matter of moments, though, the noise and confusion faded into the distance, and we were well past small talk and deep into life issues. From the tears in her eyes, I could tell Linda really cared about every word I shared.

Like many successful women, Linda often gets pegged as a crisp, well-organized executive who knows how to drive for results. In my view, that's only part of who Linda is. Yes, she rose to the top of Wells Fargo Bank by being effective. But down deep, she has a huge heart – particularly for young women in need.

Today she's the executive director of a fast-growing international ministry that serves young women dealing with addictions, eating disorders and abuse. But that role often keeps her insulated from the pain and the triumph in the lives of these women. She has given up so many perks of the executive life that I was curious what had captured her heart about giving her second half to serving these women.

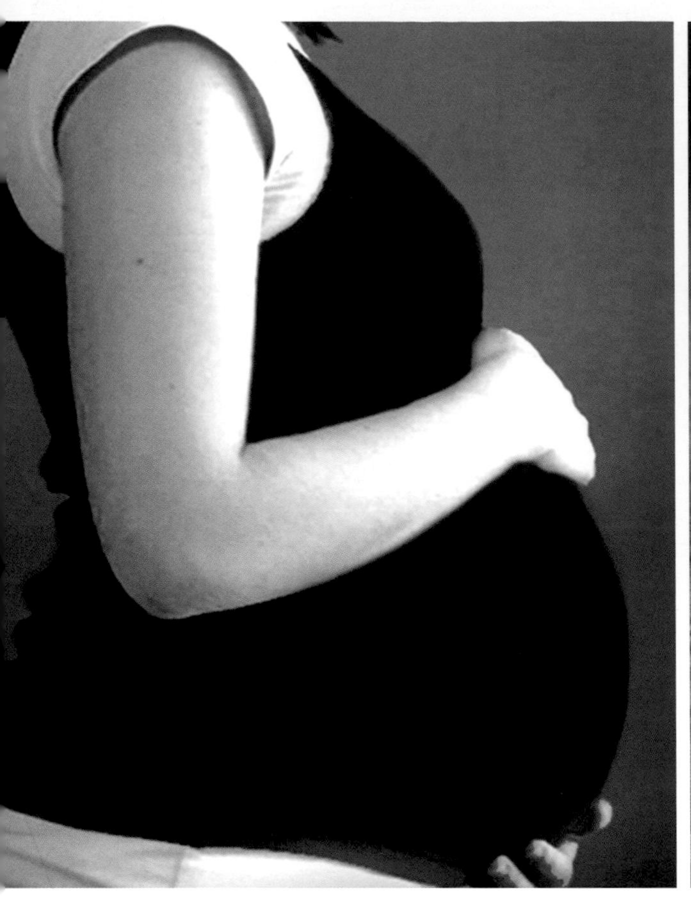

"I reached over and I gave her mom a hug, and I said it's going to be OK. We're going to love your daughter as much as you love your daughter."

As she looked across the coffee shop and into the distance, she told me about the first time she greeted a family as they dropped off their daughter at a Mercy Ministries home. The mom, dad and daughter looked worn down, physically and emotionally. Linda could see the sense of hopelessness in their faces as they hauled in baggage filled with pain: An unexpected pregnancy? Depression? Addiction? Abuse? Linda couldn't be sure, but they were walking right toward her and the inevitable interaction caused her to pause. It wasn't her job, but she knew in that moment she had to greet them.

"I thought, 'I've got to let them know what we're about,'" Linda says.

So she introduced herself in a nice, formal handshake way, then opened up her heart. "It's OK to cry," she told the young girl. "We're going to cry with you. We're going to get you through this."

"I gave her a big hug, and she started sobbing," Linda says. "I reached over and I gave her mom a hug, and I said, 'It's going to be OK. We're going to love your daughter as much as you love your daughter.' She cried, and she said, 'Oh thank you so much.'"

Linda sometimes feels her work life lacks pizzazz, and that used to bother her. "What I do is the stuff others don't want to do," she says. "I keep lists. I follow up on stuff. At Wells Fargo I was known as the great nag." So Linda keeps a photo album filled with images of women like the one she greeted that day. Each picture reminds her that she's right where she's meant to be for the second half of her life.

"I just make sure all the bills are paid, everybody has a paycheck, the lights stay on, and the food comes in," Linda says. "But when you have those kinds of moments it's like ... well, you don't lose those memories."

So how'd she launch into this second half adventure? Linda grew up in a broken home, got a degree in speech communications because it didn't require math, married and planned to work until she had children. But her career with Wells Fargo took her to unexpected heights. "It blew me away, to do as well as I did," she says. "I never wanted it, but once you get in the wheel of it, it's just an engine."

Then she made an unusual decision that inexplicably led to a life-changing second-half career: She dumped the Minnesota Vikings. It sounds crazy, of course, but that's where it started. Linda and her family lived in Minneapolis, so they were Vikings fans. But one day a star player landed in trouble for mistreating the meter maid in the street. Linda's son, watching it on the news, thought it was "cool" and Linda didn't. Looking for better role models, as a family, they dumped the Vikings and adopted the Tennessee Titans. As she began to follow her new team, she noticed its head coach was connected to Mercy Ministries.

Having gone through such brokenness in her own childhood, she was moved to tears by "seeing that there is someplace for people to get their life aligned with the Lord."

Linda and her husband, David, began donating to the ministry and later she volunteered on projects she could work on from Minnesota. Then the founder of Mercy Ministry, Nancy Alcorn, asked Linda to join their team as COO. It was a perfect fit for her gifts and her 15 years of corporate experience.

"The administrative gifting that I bring to Mercy Ministry really supports

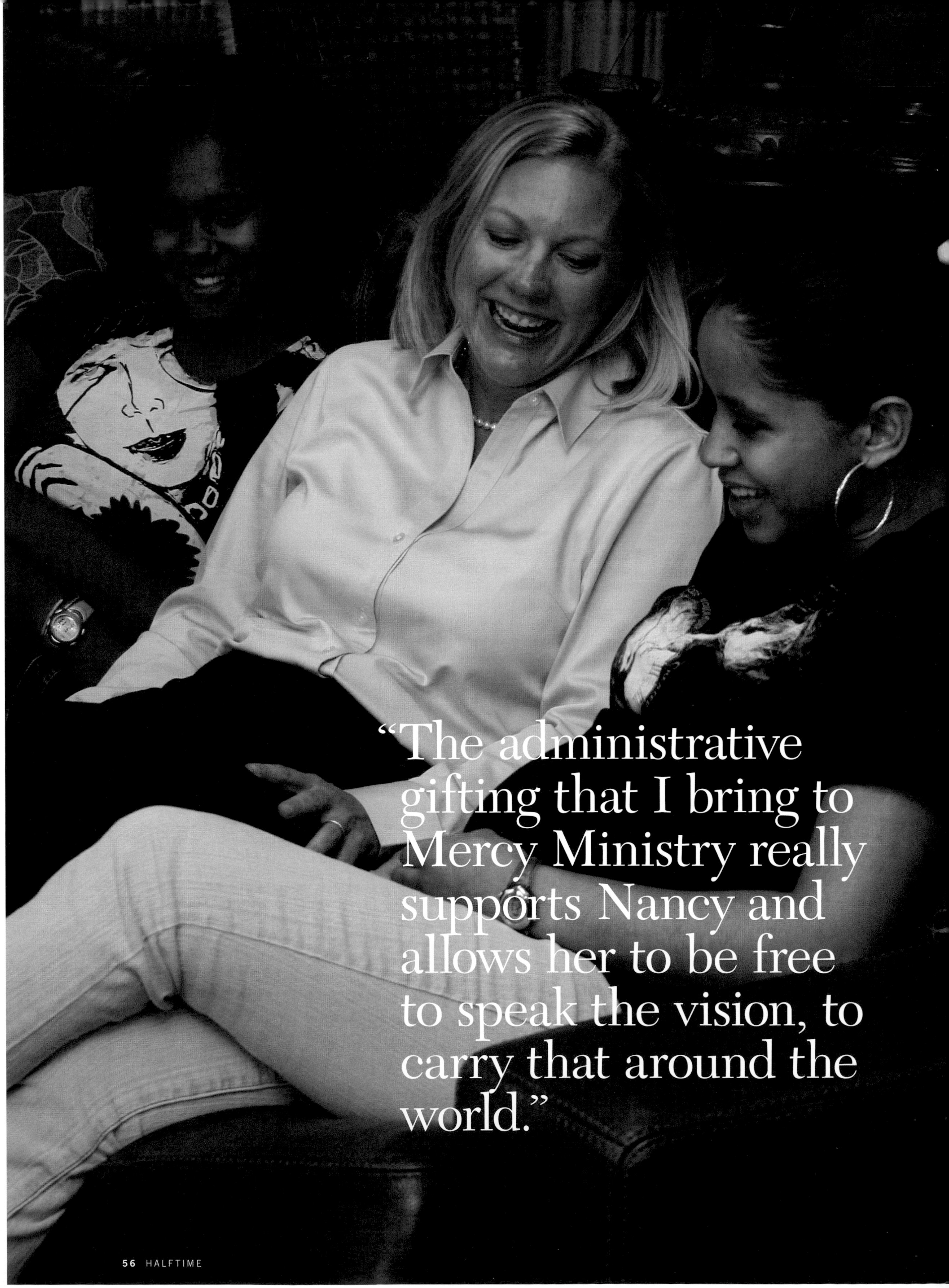

"The administrative gifting that I bring to Mercy Ministry really supports Nancy and allows her to be free to speak the vision, to carry that around the world."

Nancy and allows her to be free to speak the vision, to carry that around the world," Linda says.

There was a time when Linda hated her gifts. She saw her knack for managing projects and people as "boring" and lacking the glamour she saw attached to the work of so many other executives.

Then one day at work an employee walked into Linda's corner office asking to go home. She was struggling with a decision about having an abortion. The single mom already had three children, and she told Linda she couldn't afford another. Linda shut the door, and gave her not only her time but her heart. "I want you to pray, seek whatever higher power you believe in," she told her. "And I want you to really reflect on whether or not it's right to stop this pregnancy." The company had supported the woman through her last pregnancy, and Linda assured her that she'd get that support again if she had this child. Then she promised to still love her no matter what decision she made.

The woman had the baby and still stays in contact with Linda, who encouraged her to go back to school and finish her college degree. For Linda, the experience opened her eyes to the impact she can have regardless of how much pizzazz her daily tasks involve.

"I'm going to be the person behind the scenes, working one-on-one, kicking people in the pants to be a better employee," she says. "This is where I shine; I will not shine on the stage."

Linda gets plenty of satisfaction from seeing others take the stage, especially the women who come through Mercy's program and tell their stories during a graduation ceremony.

"They share the journey that they were on and the journey they went through at Mercy, where God transformed their lives and hope was restored in their hearts. They talk through that in front of their family, the staff, and they are just so grateful," Linda says. "There are very few dry eyes. Not tears of sorrow. It's just that you see how powerful God can be in our lives if we let Him."

There's even more impact from Linda's second-half adventure than you can see in these photos: The impact on her own family. After all, her kids saw their dad put the needs and calling of his wife ahead of his own. And their mom has modeled for them that life isn't all about her (or them), but about helping others.

"I brought my son to a Mercy graduation, and he left halfway through the testimonies," she says. "He said, 'Mom, I've got to go outside,' and he just lost it. He started crying and said, 'Mom that's way more than I thought. That's more than I realized these girls went through.'"

That's a lasting legacy that Linda simply can't buy for her kids – she had to model it. HT

For additional information and helpful Web links related to Linda's journey from success to significance, visit www.halftime.org/thesecondhalf and click on her name.

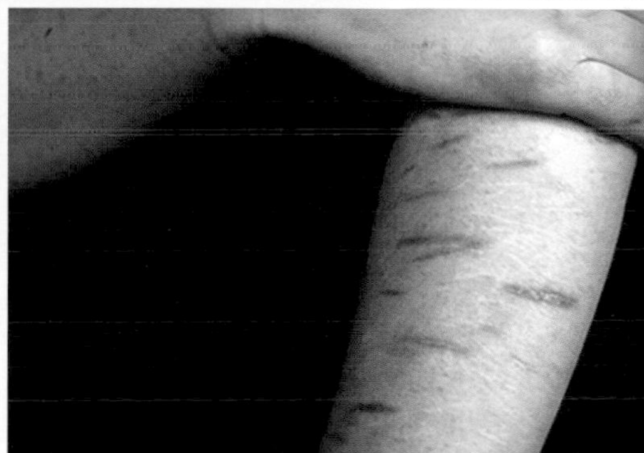

Giving the world a smile

DR. PHILLIP KEMP

Dr. Phillip Kemp sat in the back at a Halftime event, his arms crossed as he listened intently to the program. He wore an expression I've come to recognize, an expression that says, "Is this Halftime thing really for me?"

So I asked him that day what was going through his mind.

As a relatively young dentist, Phillip had a successful practice in a well-to-do Nashville suburb, but he was in no position to retire on his savings and start or join a nonprofit. He was wondering how a dentist gives back in a meaningful way. Besides, he thought, isn't just caring for people's teeth a pretty significant life? Great questions, and not so easy to answer. As it turned out, he didn't have to leave his practice or move to a poor country. His platform of dentistry became a powerful launching pad for serving others – for serving aspiring dentists and for serving the poor and broken-hearted.

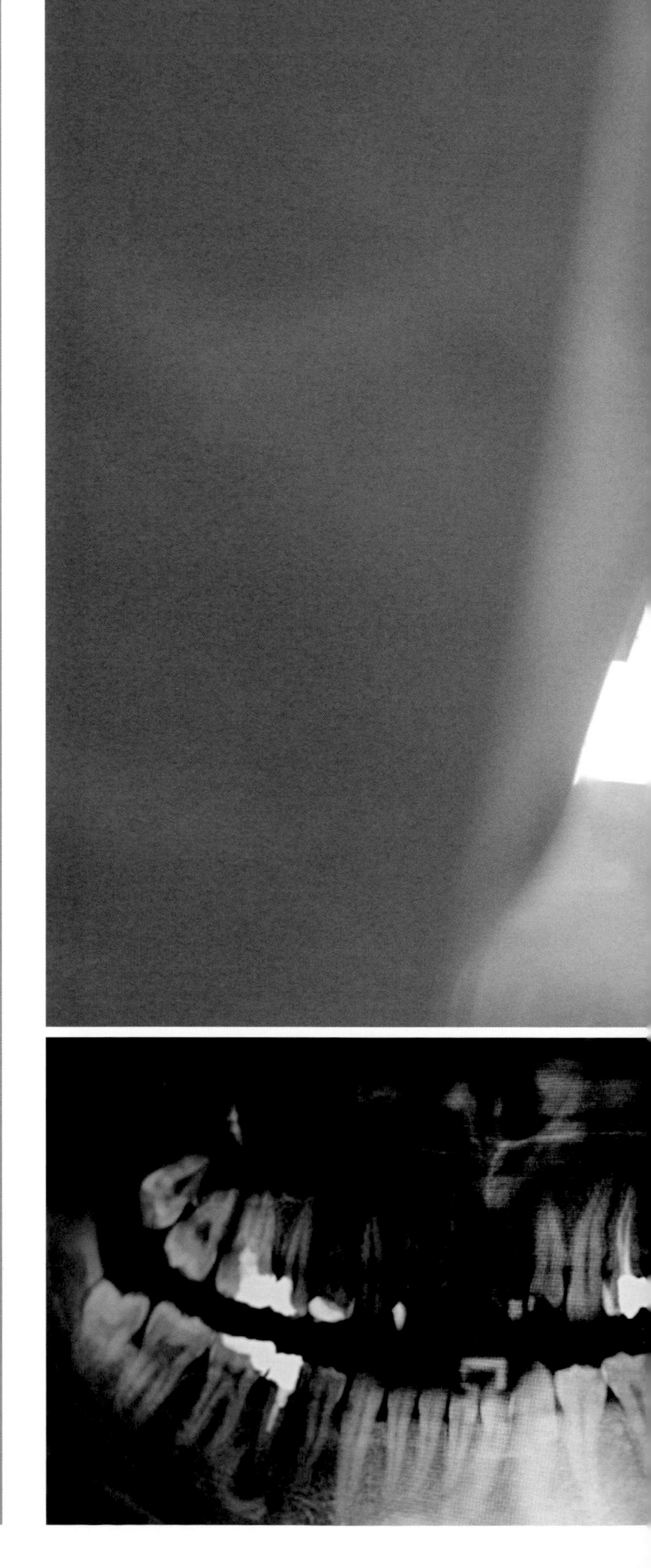

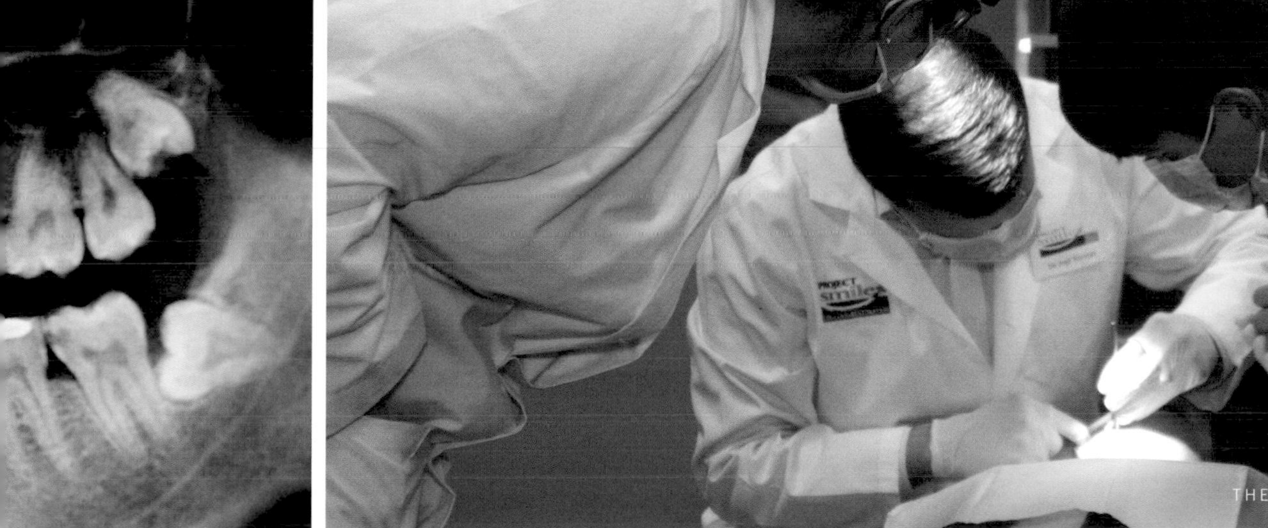

"I feel like God's called me to the mission field, which is here in this office in Brentwood, Tenn.," Phillip says.

Phillip's quest to match his passions and gifts with the needs of others led to a creative program that others now want to replicate across the country and around the world.

Most Fridays, Phillip and his staff volunteer to treat patients who can't afford care, usually women who are in nearby recovery programs such at the Hope Center or Mercy Ministries (see Linda Hood's story on page 52). Through neglect or abuse, these women often require significant cosmetic dental work as they rebuild their self-esteem and find their way back into society.

What makes his second-half calling unique and its impact more powerful, however, is that it's more than just providing free dental care to the needy. It has leverage because in the process he's mentoring student dentists and modeling for them the idea that the most rewarding practice is bigger than tooth care and includes the deepest heart-needs of your patients.

Phillip brings in a rotation of dental students from his alma mater who witness and assist on complex procedures they may never get a chance to see in their academic environment.

"I've always had a desire to mentor and teach young dentists and give back," Phillip says. "This whole process has been a culmination of that dream."

It started with Phillip going back to his dental school and beginning a conversation with the dean about how he could serve them. In short order the students were coming to his office. His credibility has grown in the university, and now he's in a position to grow the program across the Nashville area.

As these students look over his shoulder and learn the latest procedures, they get to hear from his heart about why his life's passion is to serve these people. He lifts their vision above building a practice that creates wealth to a practice that transforms lives. He calls them into a higher story for their profession.

"In school, they're taught it's just the tooth: 'Here it's the tooth attached to this person. This is what you fix,'" Phillip says. "We take it from the whole heart aspect that the tooth is just a means … and that whole care really serves the heart of the patient. That's when they start saying, 'Oh wow! I can have this kind of impact with what we do on a daily basis.'"

And the university benefits, too, says Phillip. "The dean sees it as something they can't provide, and it's a huge benefit to the students."

On a more regional basis, he hopes to start a training center and clinic that provides low- or no-cost services while teaching dental students, moving the program beyond his office so that it can operate more than just one day a week.

This program also has had a profound impact on Phillip's staff. When it first started, Phillip paid his staff for their work each Friday and he volunteered his time. Before long, as they saw the impact they were having, his staff members began coming to him one by one, offering to give back their salaries for that day. Eventually, they just asked not to be paid, even though he's more than willing to make that a cost of providing the service.

The patients, many of whom saw their mouths as a focal point of depression, often find the procedures life-changing. Phillip keeps the letters that inevitably come, sharing them all with his staff, his wife and his four children.

One note in particular touched his heart. It came from a girl enrolled in a treatment program at Mercy Ministries. Her mouth looked like a jack-o-lantern's. The teeth that weren't missing, Phillip said, were "horrible." And most of her oral problems weren't from neglect, which meant she'd been living with them all her life.

"The teeth that weren't missing were horrible. From the time she was young until we treated her, she was just berated unmercifully, even by people in her family and friends at school."

"From the time she was young until we treated her, she was just berated unmercifully, even by people in her family and friends at school," Phillip recounts. "She talked about how the work that was done on her smile not only restored her self-esteem, but her faith in men."

When Phillip talks about the program offering "life, love and restoration," he's not just talking about restoring healthy teeth and smiles. "It's restoration of lives," he says. "This girl really communicated that."

Living a second half of significance always involves risk and sacrifice, but these stories re-affirm for Phillip that giving his time and talent, not to mention sacrificing a day's pay, is easily worth the price. Indeed, Phillip and his wife Rhonda hardly see it as a sacrifice but as "the least" they can do.

"We just feel like, as a family, if we're not doing this then we're not serving God," Phillip says. "Taking off a few Fridays to do this is just a drop in the bucket. It's like the guy walking on the shore and throwing the starfish in. I don't feel like we do enough."

That's why it's so amazing to see how God is using it for something much, much bigger than Phillip ever envisioned. And as a result of his speaking engagements at dental conferences, dentists and universities are replicating this strategy in other communities.

"The legacy of where I think God is calling me to be is a lot more about my ability to impact the profession," Phillip says. "It's truly more about the practitioner than the people we practice on. It's not the treatment we do, but it's what we do with the treatment providers. I truly think and feel that we're on the cusp of just this whole movement of educating and raising up people to give back. That is going to impact a tremendous amount of people in the next 20 years." HT

For additional information and helpful Web links related to Phillip's journey from success to significance, visit www.halftime.org/thesecondhalf and click on his name.

DAWSON

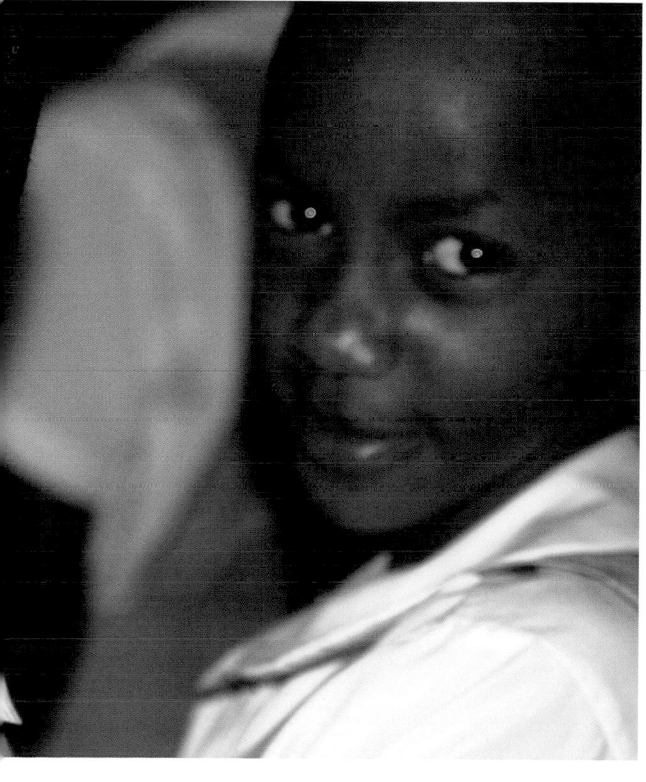

From the Rock to Rwanda

DABBS CAVIN AND DALE DAWSON

Soccer balls bounced around in the back seat of Dabbs Cavin's 10-year-old Volvo, one of many signs of family activity that belied his role as a bank president.

His boyish face it seemed was always on the verge of laughter, yet he wore an air of confidence that fit like a well-tailored suit on his 6-foot-3 frame.

Fun-loving and passionate about relationships; serious and aggressive about pursuing large-scale objectives. Those aren't contradictions. Those are the marks of a man who models what it means to enjoy life while still giving himself to serious endeavors – like starting a microfinance bank in Rwanda with his friend Dale Dawson.

A former investment banker and dealmaker, Dale spent much of his first half hooked on the drug of adrenalin. Then the deals stopped producing the thrill, and the drive to succeed began to wane. Today he's fallen in love with Rwanda, of all places.

Dale, Dabbs and their spouses have traveled some common roads on a second-half adventure that's helping break the cycle of poverty for thousands of families in a country with a tortured past but a promising future.

Dale primarily worked to organize, mobilize and connect resources as part of Opportunity International's efforts to charter a commercial bank in Rwanda that would focus on microfinance. Dabbs and his wife Mary, meanwhile, moved their family to Rwanda in 2006 so he could use his banking experience to help launch the project. By partnering with World Relief and Hope International, two organizations already established in Rwanda, Urwego Opportunity Bank opened with a portfolio of nearly 30,000 loans and nearly 3,000 savings clients.

"We could take the systems and processes – the opportunities we had – and combine that with the work that already had been done by World Relief and Hope to really scale up the bank at a much faster rate than what we would have been able to had we gone in on our own," says Dabbs, who was the bank's CEO.

So how does it work? A loan of even $70 to a poor single mom allows her to buy a sewing machine and some cloth so she can make wedding dresses for rent, or used shoes in bulk that she can repair and sell, or a cow for a small farm. "There were literally thousands of different kinds of businesses that people were able to start with their loans," Dabbs says. Borrowers meet in groups, and together they learn business skills and hold each other accountable – if someone doesn't show up with an interest payment, the rest of the group is responsible for it.

Over time, they pay off their loans and often take new, larger loans. And as they grow their businesses, they improve their quality of life – replacing mud floors with stone, paying tuition so their children can go to school, buying essential medicines – while becoming leaders in their towns and models for other young women. With a little help, they've broken the cycle of poverty. That's not theory. I have met these women and heard their stories – it works.

"Most people in developing countries do not have that kind of support network or accountability or discipline in their lives," Dale says. "When you bring that in there … then they begin to develop a sense of purpose, a sense of confidence, and a sense that things are doable. You see transformation. You see people's hope and confidence and dignity become restored. … It's a wonder to watch. When somebody's been through several of these cycles in two or three years, it's the confidence and the dignity they have, the pride they have in what they've accomplished. That's what's really exciting."

The Dawsons and Cavins share similar professional histories and were friends in Little Rock, Ark., before they all became invested in Rwanda, but they took very different paths to such an unlikely destination. Dale's wife Judi was Mary's partner as insti-

Dale, Dabbs and their spouses have traveled some common roads on a second-half adventure that's helping break the cycle of poverty for thousands of families in a country with a tortured past but a promising future.

tutional brokers at Stephens Inc., where Dale once was head of investment banking. But for Dabbs and Mary, pulling up roots and moving to Rwanda for one and a half years was a reaction to a long-time pursuit of how to live out their faith, while Dale and Judi developed their passion for significance a little later in life.

"Mary and I together have wanted to step out and serve the Lord, especially in ways that benefit the extreme poor, and that's been something that we've had on our hearts for a long time," Dabbs says. "A lot of times, one spouse or the other really doesn't realize they're not being prayerful enough or hopeful enough for God's call and mercy and grace in their lives, and they end up building walls that limit their abilities and opportunities to serve. My wife has been one who wants to embrace opportunities to serve the Lord, even if that means a sacrifice."

When the prospect of moving to Rwanda emerged, Mary was all over it. They took their two children, and Mary helped found an international school while Dabbs helped launch the bank. She and Dabbs also opened their home three or four nights a week for social events involving a wide spectrum of people who were in Rwanda working on different projects.

"Ultimately, our house became a place where people were connected," Dabbs says. "We ended up becoming kind of the hub for that. ... So while we were there, we had over 120 people stay at our home for as long as six weeks, and I believe Mary served over 1,500 meals. That was a lot of fun because people were coming and staying, and, of course, you'd stay up until late in the night as we talked about how we could better help the poor and how we can share the love of Jesus with others. It was exciting."

Finding themselves in Rwanda helping connect missionaries and government officials and business leaders came as a natural next step in life for Dabbs and Mary – the very type of opportunity for which they'd been praying. Dale, on the other hand, never saw it coming. His first half focused almost

The Dawsons and Cavins share similar professional histories and were friends in Little Rock before they all became invested in Rwanda, but they took very different paths to such an unlikely destination.

exclusively on building financial success, and it took a major mid-life re-evaluation for him to catch a vision for nonprofit work.

"I always wanted to be a deal guy," he says. "I always wanted to be somebody who bought businesses, who was smart, clever and driven. So from college until I was 46, that's what I did. It was all about building companies, doing deals, making money."

Dale worked in investment banking for Stephens Inc., then was CEO of a successful truck parts business. When he sold it to AutoZone, he and Judi took a year off to reassess life. She decided to be a full-time mom and he went back to Stephens, but he soon realized he lacked the same passions that drove him early in his career.

In 2002, at age 50, Dale met Anglican Bishop John Rucyahana, one of the leaders in the post-genocide change movement in Rwanda and founder of the Sonrise School to serve orphans of the genocide.

Dale and Judi knew about the school because another friend of theirs, Martha Vetter, had left Little Rock a year earlier to serve as its headmistress. Her decision to take that assignment had, in many ways, confounded Dale and Judi.

"We thought it was a terrible idea," Dale says. "She had a great ministry in Little Rock. She was single, 42 years old, and we just couldn't think of anything more life-limiting than for her to pack up and move to the middle of Africa and try to build a school for orphans. And yet, she went. We had never seen anybody surrender their life, what seemed like an obviously bad move, to do something they felt called to do."

A year later, Dale and Judi hosted a fund-raising dinner for the school, and Bishop John was one of the guests.

"I knew he was very special from that one evening," Dale says. "He was a different kind of guy. ... He was just as entrepreneurial and just as driven, just as goal-oriented as any entrepreneur I've ever met, and yet he was working for Jesus. He wasn't working to increase his net worth. I was intrigued and drawn and attracted to his passion and the purity of his motivation."

Dale began reevaluating his definition of success. "I began to think in terms of how would Jesus define success? That was a new idea for me, to look at the way Jesus lived his life. ... It had nothing to do with power. It had nothing to do with money. It had nothing to do with affluence or wealth. It had to do with love. It had to do with service to others. It had to do with using your skills for somebody else, and not for yourself. Those were all a different way to define success for me."

Before he knew it, Dale had left Stephens, was making regular trips to Rwanda and working on projects like the new bank.

"It seems completely ridiculous," he says. "It seems absurd. I had never been on a mission trip in my life. I didn't have any interest in doing mission work. I'd never been to Africa, nor did I have any interest in Africa except I thought maybe someday I'd go do a game-watching safari or something. I've never viewed myself as a missionary or a minister, nor did I have any interest in those kinds of activities, and I still don't."

But Dale still has an interest in building businesses and making deals and raising capital. And that's what he does.

"I really don't want to manage any of these institutions we're building," he says. "I'm interested in identifying a need and an opportunity, casting a vision for it, and then drawing other people into that vision and developing a strategy and a plan, and raising money and getting it started. There are thousands of details related to running a school or a business or a bank that I don't really want to do. So it's always important to me to find a leader that's going to run these institutions, because I don't want to run them. That's not my greatest strength. What's interesting to me is starting something and putting the pieces together."

That passion fit perfectly with Rwanda's vision for the future. After the genocide in the mid 1990s, Rwanda's leaders created a vision for long-term growth and stability that would make their country a model and economic driver for all of Africa. They realized, however, that to do this they would have to borrow talent from the rest of the world, both to take on certain jobs and to train Rwandans. Their strategy identified three groups – high-capacity Halftimers, faith-based professional volunteers and academics – as those most qualified and most motivated to help. Dale and Dabbs fit nicely in that mix.

"My personal mission, which is to build a bridge from here to Rwanda and transform lives at both ends, calls me to be that person on the bridge that's helping to mobilize that borrowed talent and bring it to Rwanda," Dale says.

Rwanda remains a country ripe with struggles, but Dale and Dabbs see progress and hope. They see it in the successes of the people who have taken out micro-loans, and they see it in the next generation leaders who are progressing through the schools and internships and other programs now being established.

"That generation of young people – six, seven, eight years from now when they're in their 20s – will drive the advancement of Rwanda as a demonstration to all of Africa that Africa can be first world, that they can be world class," Dale says. "That's what I want to see." HT

For additional information and helpful Web links related to Dale and Dabb's journeys from success to significance (as well as Todd Brogdoni, who also moved to Rwanda to be the CFO), visit www.halftime.org/thesecondhalf and click on their names.

Integrity
Respect

Life in the intersection

PAUL CHOU

I'll never forget the conversation Paul Chou and I had one afternoon while driving through the streets of Beijing.

As I listened to my brilliant friend talk, one conclusion became unavoidable: His mind was a lot like the traffic – speeding around in every direction, weaving in and out.

Paul's not offended by the characterization. He's a unique blend of scientist and visionary, a reality that drove his entrepreneurial success and that still keeps him jumping from big idea to big idea. It's a reality that's led to big-time results – with his companies, with his philanthropic foundation and with his work in recent years building an organization in China.

Paul started as an engineer in the Bell Laboratories and later founded several successful software companies in the United States. Early in his career, his wife Alice and a former pastor helped him see that business was more than just a career – it was his "calling." As he approached Halftime, he looked for ways to pass that along to the next generation. So he set out to mentor younger Asian Americans, not Chinese nationals. He knew the challenges they faced because they had different traditions and came from different cultures. And he wanted to model what it looked like to be a global businessman of character.

In America, he and Alice founded the L2 Foundation to promote "leadership and legacy" among Asian Americans. In China they are investing in education, and in time Paul became more involved in Junior Achievement China. They split their time now between homes in Beijing and Raleigh, N.C.

Paul, a quiet man who loves China and, despite the noise and intense traffic, loves Beijing, long ago recognized the country's potential in the world economy. Since 1993, his long-term vision has included creating models of the core values and ethics essential for the free-market economy to work as it emerges in China.

"At age 47 I was able to have the financial freedom to start to look at my second half and what I should be doing," Paul says. "I believe that I'm in a unique position where I received a family upbringing that showed me what China is, what my homeland is, so there is a romantic love for China. The combination of who I am, my faith and the passion for China caused me to develop a game plan to use my resources and my talents to serve China."

It's also led to bouts with frustration bordering on discouragement, because seeing how the future can look, even when the vision is bright, often means interacting with those who can't see it and refuse to embrace it.

And that's exactly where Alice shines. She's more of a linear thinker, an effective implementer. Paul had the vision back in 1993 for bringing Junior Achievement to a country that at the time had very little experience with nonprofits. But he and Alice supported the effort mainly by sending checks. When the program floundered, Alice stepped in and spent three years righting the organizational ship, then handed it to her husband so he could take it to new heights. In the process, the two became closer than ever.

"My scattered mind, and my dreams and visionary skills – she can understand them," Paul says. "She basically comes along and affirms me. It's not easy for her to listen to me, to understand me, to witness my frustration, ... to see me struggling trying to express what I see in the future ... so she has learned how to leverage me, to complement me, to make sure that I can complete what I have started, to encourage me."

Paul grew up outside of China, but he knows well the history of China – the 5,000 years of empirical rule, the eight-year invasion by Japan, the civil war, the turn to communism, and more recent experiments in economic reform. "I live in the intersection of the old China and the new China," he says.

His vision is to be a bridge between the two.

"Our core value in Junior Achievement China is that we believe that to be a successful global businessman or woman one must first have excellent character and secondly performance," he says. "When these two things intersect it produces trust-

"I live in the intersection of the old China and the new China."

worthiness of that person. Trustworthiness is the intimacy of the relationship, so, therefore, business is about relationship. In that relationship, it's about trust, and that's the engine behind great companies and behind great business leaders."

These ideas are still new in China, where a centrally planned economy kept entrepreneurial spirits dormant for decades. Seeing businessmen as something more than crooked merchants is new, and the basic ideas of personal ownership, volunteerism and philanthropy are still ideas in their infancy.

"I model for them what it looks like to give back to society," Paul says. "Most of the Chinese, when they give back to society, if they do, it's mostly what you call emotional giving as opposed to venture philanthropy, where we don't just write checks, we want to do deals that have leverage and build organizational capacity."

With a staff of 28 and growing, JA China provides free business and financial education to more than 350,000 young people and will reach 1 million students over the next three years. And in a country where people aren't accustomed to giving things away – because they aren't used to owning anything that they could give – JA China now has more than 25,000 volunteers. The volunteers assist with a variety of programs, including a national competition that challenges students to create a viable business.

"Through the competition they will receive an award and seed money to start their business," says Paul. "A group of high-schoolers form a company, write a business plan, issue stock, raise the capital, form their organization – president, vice president, manufacturing, sales, finance, R & D. A real company on campus. They select a product and design and manufacture, then go sell. They'll learn how to deal with the bank. They'll talk about corporate social responsibility."

One of Paul's favorite examples of JA China's success involves a high school student who started a waste management company around the idea of collecting recyclables and selling them to a larger company in Beijing.

"He went to Boeing, who is the sponsor of the program, to pick up the Coca-Cola and water bottles," Paul says. "He showed up and they had two truckloads of empty bottles for him. He came to pick them up on his bicycle."

Later, a government-sponsored television program promoting philanthropy included a feature on the young entrepreneur. Of the six programs featured, JA China was the only one that wasn't government-owned. The 17-year-old president of a waste management student company sat next to the president of Boeing's China division and had a dialogue on equal footing, almost as if they were peers, talking about business as presidents of a company – passionate, dedicated, confident.

"That young man is evidence of the future," Paul says. "We're going to see hundreds if not thousands of young people working hard to create wealth, 1.4 billion Chinese today working together to create wealth. The government recognizes the importance of character, moral values for all of these people. The government recognizes that we cannot just develop a market economy without core values and moral values behind it."

"I'm very optimistic about the future of China. They do recognize the need, and they are fast learners. China is in transition, constantly learning, applying, and in transition, learning, applying, and then in transition again. I hope that we, from our core values, our faith, that we can bring (value) to China, to work along next to her, to affirm her and welcome her."

Paul and Alice now work closely together to make this vision a reality, and it's drawn them closer as a couple.

"Sometimes Halftime is a lot about what you do – the project you do or the adventure you're in – but really it's a way for God to bring the two of us together even more in our life as a couple," Alice says. "In our story, that's what is happening, that through this, God has shown us so much about our hearts and our relationship as a couple and our need to really uphold each other." HT

For additional information and helpful Web links related to Paul's journey from success to significance, visit www.halftime.org/thesecondhalf and click on his name.

Marketing a new message

PAULA DUMAS

Many times we need an organizational platform for our second-half adventures. Paula Dumas had a blast in her first half learning the art of marketing from some of America's best: Frito Lay, CNN, Apple, Disney and Kodak.

After taking a year off to focus on family, she had decided to re-enter the marketplace and her searching boiled down to two organizations.

On the one had, there was a job she "had absolutely jumped through hoops for." She had passed all the IQ testing and the background checks. The company had one of the world's leading brands, and it offered her an "astronomical salary" with a "Porsche in the color of my choice." (As someone who loves horsepower, the Porsche sounded pretty tempting to me.) On the other hand, there was a job with FamilyLife, a nonprofit that could seemingly offer just a fraction of the other job.

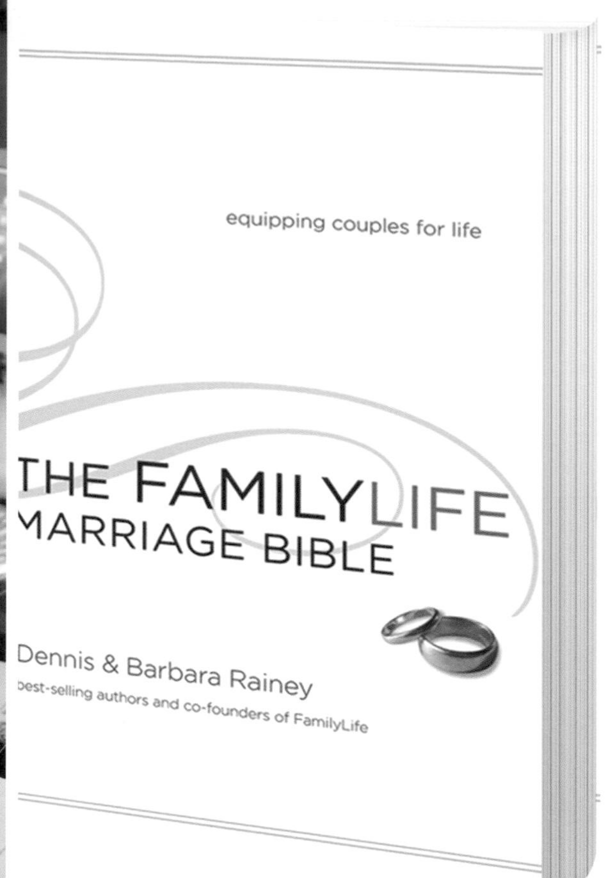

Many Halftimers are having measurable ministry impact in a high-profile job inside corporate America, but Paula had zoomed down that road before and she knew where she now needed to go. Earlier that year, at a Halftime event that I facilitated in Atlanta, she was among a couple dozen marketplace leaders we were introducing to innovative ministries impacting their city. At that event, she says, she felt a clear longing for something more than just another job – she was looking for a sense of calling.

"Do I really want to help save people's marriages so that they can have a solid foundation for raising kids and know how to apply God's word in their family life?" she asked herself. "Or should I sell them another car or soft drink that they really don't need to get by in life? It was just sort of a very simple decision at that point in time. ... It would be nothing short of greedy to go after the other opportunity, unless I thought I could do great ministry in that environment, but I didn't have any indication that would be true."

Paula realized her professional career – the stresses it had heaped on her family as well as the high-level training and broad experiences that came with success – had prepared her perfectly to lead the marketing efforts for FamilyLife. But that wasn't something she envisioned starting out.

"Early on, I had sort of big-scale ambitions," she says. "I wanted to reach the nation and reach the world, and so I was really interested in organizations that had a very broad distribution and a strong commercial brand. Ministry was not on my radar except on a personal level."

In her 20s, fresh out of college and working for Frito-Lay, Paula managed a $70 million ad budget with three agencies at her disposal. Success begot opportunity, and she went to work for CNN. She also got married, and soon she began wrestling with the conflicts of balancing marriage, family and a demanding career in a demanding industry.

"Our marriage was tested big time," she says. "We nearly split up in that very first year, but we stuck it out. It just gets better and better each year, only after we endured some very early trials, mostly brought on by my career and the industry I was in."

Paula left CNN for Apple and later went to Disney, where she helped launch a startup division that would manage the corporation's global partnerships.

With every move, Paula learned more about her profession and continued to reach her goals of impacting broad audiences across the world. When her children came along, however, the career-family tensions increased. Paula left Disney for a more family friendly work environment offered at Kodak. But success again begot opportunities, and soon she found herself responding more to the needs of the corporation and less to the needs of her husband and children.

"That was my own failure to set boundaries," she says. "I think God really called me to live out my values and demonstrate my faith, and I wasn't doing it."

The defining moment came after she returned from a four-day business trip. She had called home one night during the trip, and her then 7-year-old son had told her that he had competed in his first golf tournament and won. "Then I came home and found that he hadn't even placed and that he had lied to me," Paula says. "I just

"The most basic unit of civilization – the family – is in crisis, and needs help now. That's a massive challenge."

cried because I thought it was so sad that my son would feel the need to get my approval on something like that, and I thought: 'This is just not right.'"

Paula made a decision to leave Kodak, but was able to stay another three years under a renegotiated agreement that made her the company's only part-time vice president. Soon she began to value the things she did away from work more than the things she did at work.

"The job became less satisfying as my work in ministry became more satisfying, and suddenly I realized that I was having an impact on people's lives in my neighborhood, in my women's group and in my church that my lack of time and margin never allowed," she says. "And I definitely was able to serve and love my kids and help my husband in more ways than I ever could before. Life became more satisfying, even with less income and career prestige."

Paula finally left Kodak and spent even more time with her family, while also taking on some consulting projects for her church and for corporations around her home in Atlanta.

FamilyLife provided a platform for Paula to re-enter the marketplace with an organization led by Dennis and Barbara Rainey that truly valued family. "FamilyLife actually wanted me to be home to meet the school bus, to be the wife and mom I yearned to be." The ministry, based in Little Rock, Ark., allowed her to take on the role of Chief Marketing Officer while staying in Atlanta, where her husband's small business is based.

She quickly adjusted to the smaller budgets while embracing what she came to see as a bigger vision.

"I had spent so much of my career dealing with change on a mass level," Paula says. "The most basic unit of civilization – the family – is in crisis, and needs help now. That's a massive challenge."

Yet, in terms of scalability, FamilyLife provides an organizational platform for Paula to leverage her marketing skills for a global impact. It's a well-run organization that already touches millions of families – more than 80,000 people experience one of their *Weekend To Remember* conferences each year, and for most of them it will change their marriage forever. Millions listen each week to their radio program and use their resources to find help and hope for their own families. And with her marketing skills, they can impact "even more" with the Truth.

Could it be that she was uniquely prepared for this role and that, as wonderful as her first half was, her greatest impact and most fun adventures remain ahead?

"Even though we have a much smaller budget to work with than some of the other companies that I've worked for," she says, "our playing field is even greater. We still have the world to reach, and it's a daunting opportunity to do that." HT

For additional information and helpful Web links related to Paula's journey from success to significance, visit www.halftime.org/thesecondhalf and click on her name.

Fueling a passion

MIKE FOX

It was the perfect evening, at least in my book. In a gracious, old country club in Kansas City, a group of successful men and women sat beneath soft lighting,

enjoying the wonderful food and sharing their common desire for getting more out of their second half – more impact and more adventure.

And they wanted to pursue it together.

I speak to about 100 different groups of men and women like this every year, so I have learned to read faces. That night as I scanned the crowd, something in the smile of Beth Fox drew me into her world. She had a certain energy and joy that just bubbled to the surface. Turns out, Mike and Beth Fox were at my table during dinner, so I want to share their story with you.

Beth knew her husband's past, but she had an intuition about his future. Many times a guy's wife can sense that he needs to make a change in midlife long before he even sees it coming (and the smart guys stop and listen). She knew Mike's over-developed work ethic had provided a pathway out of his family poverty but left him without the anchors to sustain a healthy first marriage or career. She also knew he had since discovered those anchors and was making the most of his second chances – in his faith journey, in his revived career and in his marriage to her. So as Mike packed for an adventure that would take him

ONGEBOB

well outside of his comfort zone, and halfway around the world, Beth anticipated that he wouldn't return the same.

Mike, who seldom took vacations and had never gone on a "mission" trip, wasn't sure what to expect when he agreed to visit a shelter he and Beth had funded for some orphans in Southeast Asia. So Beth, who'd taken many such excursions, made a point to personalize the new Bible she bought him for the trip.

"There was a note in there that I know I've read 10 times," Mike says. "The gist of the note is: 'You're embarking on a journey, Mike, and we don't know where you're going and we don't know how God is going to use you. But wherever it is, I'm there 100 percent in support. I've never been so proud of you. I've never been so excited about our future.' And there it was in a note in an envelope tucked in the Bible she gave me to take on this trip. It's still in there."

That 2003 trip to the Philippines, China and Thailand became the "eye opener" that jump-started Mike's second half. While most of us don't have to change careers to pursue a second-half adventure, Mike felt that he did. By the end of that year he had quit his job with a Kansas City-based propane company, founded C3 Missions International and begun a journey toward helping orphans all over the world.

The name "C3" is not a missions' term and has nothing to do with global relief. It's short for C3H8, the chemical symbol for propane, on which Mike built his first-half success and which is now the financial platform for his second-half calling. C3 has built more then 100 homes for orphans in a dozen countries, including Thailand, Cambodia and Haiti, all in partnership with local churches that are tasked with meeting the physical, nutritional, spiritual, social and educational needs of the children.

It's fitting work for a poor kid from a rough home. Mike's mother worked in bars and married and divorced several times, but Mike saw hard work as the exit ramp from that lifestyle. He always had a job, and by age 15 he owned a gift shop that paid sales taxes and was a member of the local Chamber of Commerce. He worked his way through college, got married the day he graduated and began a career in sales.

"I had a goal, I had a track and I

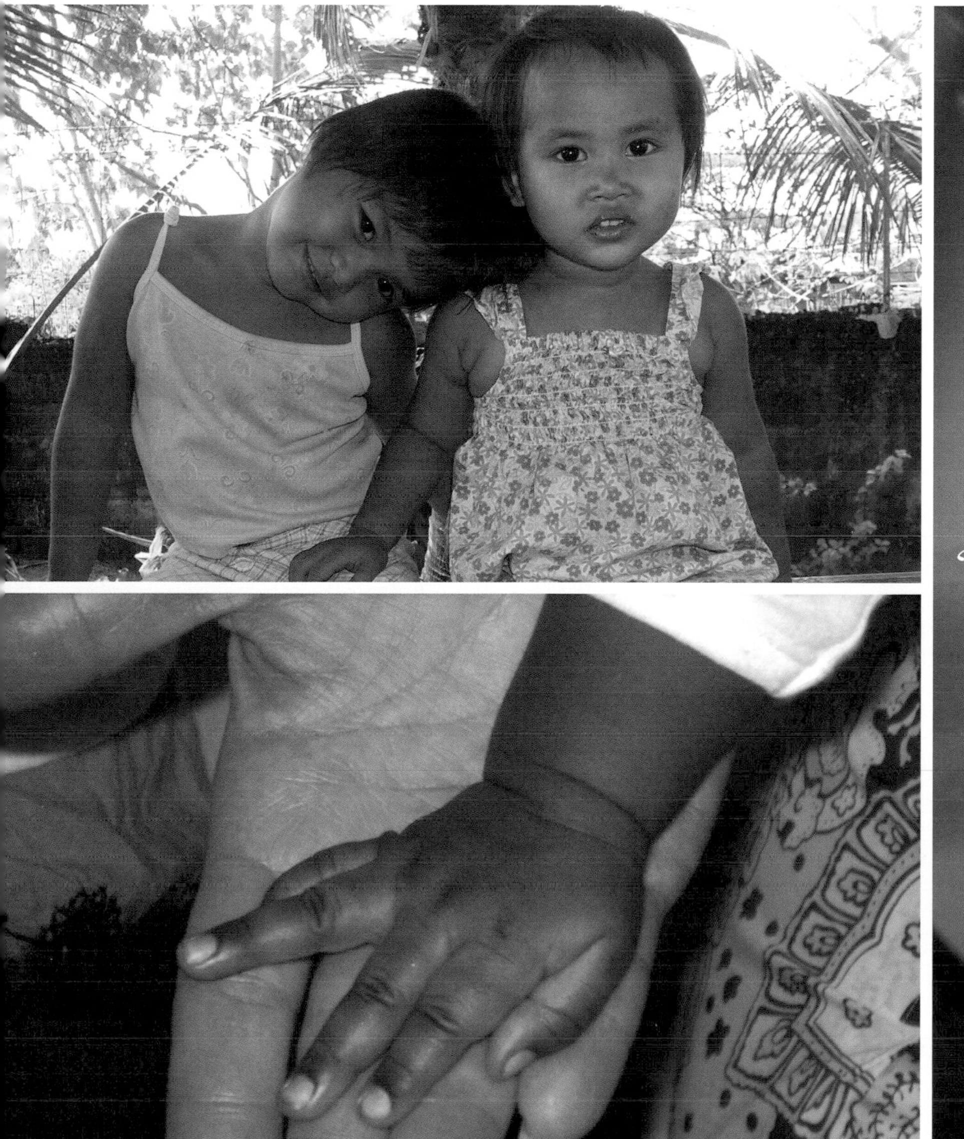

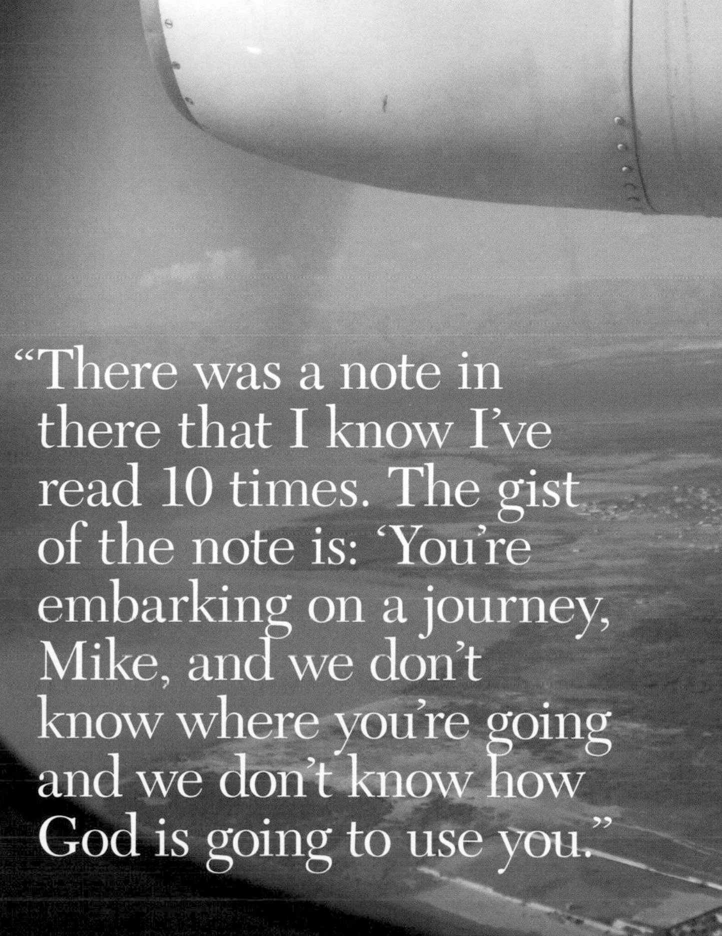

"There was a note in there that I know I've read 10 times. The gist of the note is: 'You're embarking on a journey, Mike, and we don't know where you're going and we don't know how God is going to use you."

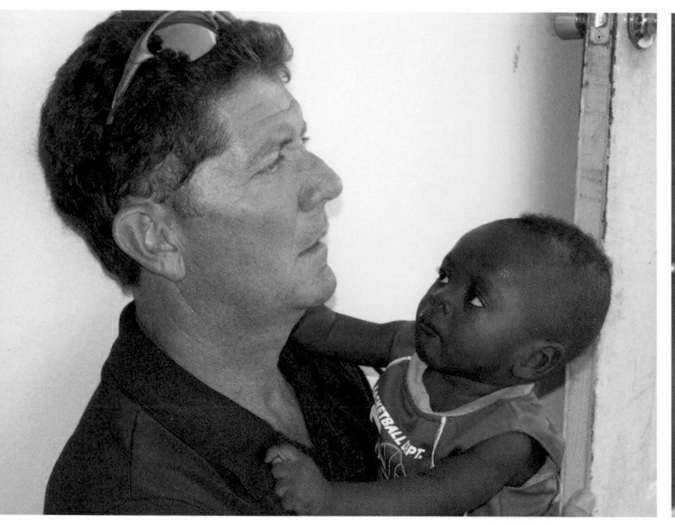

thought I knew what I was doing," he says. "I look back at it now, and I was clueless. I had no mentors, and I had no healthy relationships with Christian men. I had a demented view of the opposite sex. I had a wanderlust attitude about life. But I worked hard. So everything I did that was wrong, I justified it by saying, 'Well, I've never missed a day of work.'"

Mike worked long hours and moved up, but eventually, overconfident in his own talents, he started a company in an industry he knew nothing about. He continued to work long hours, but the company failed. So did his marriage.

"It humbled me," he says. "That was in '92, and I was on my last leg. I spent the nights living between my couch in the office, my car or my apartment."

Mike, hat in hand, went back to his former employer and slowly began to rebuild his career and his spiritual life, eventually marrying Beth and seeing her through a near-fatal brain aneurism. He also became a minority owner in Inergy, a startup propane company, and his financial condition had improved dramatically by the time he went to Southeast Asia.

During the trip, Mike visited a refugee camp between Myanmar and Thailand. He and Beth had given $750 for a shelter to house 17 orphans there, and he wanted to take the children some presents.

"The caregivers told them that there were some gifts for them, and the kids sat in rows," he says.

They weren't jumping around. They just sat quietly and patiently until it was their turn to accept Mike's gift. Each one took the gift, bowed, sat back down and held it in his or her lap. "At the end of it there were two children that didn't have presents," Mike says. "I looked in the bag, and I was out of presents. So dang, did I lose them? Did I miscount?"

No, the home had simply taken in two more children. "So here I was trying to boastfully show who I was by giving presents, and there are two children that I've broken their hearts. Did they cry? No! Were they upset? No! Did they ask

"…we're going to go to Haiti and spend 72 hours with these kids. She can't wait."

for anything? No, they just sat there smiling. All they wanted to do was sing and dance for me, all of them."

Mike asked the caregiver if there were a lot these children who didn't have shelter. "She looked at me like I was from off the planet, and she said there are 5,000 children in this camp that don't have a place, that nobody cares for. There are 50,000 children living up and down that border between Thailand and Myanmar."

In a flash, Mike knew he had to do more. He realized he didn't need more money or a bigger house or nicer cars. "I had it all," he says. "So, more money? I wasn't even spending what I had."

He returned to Kansas City, talked it over with his partners and left the company.

Wisely, the normally hard-charging businessman did something out of character for him: He intentionally moved slowly. "I didn't come home and immediately say, 'I want off this train, because I'm going to get on this new train that's going to go the other direction.' It was a process that I had to work through, and I'm glad I did because it made it more real."

Beth embraced C3 from the beginning, but her involvement really grew after they became empty-nesters. "I couldn't make it up how wonderful it is to travel with your wife – Thursday we're going to tag up with about 15 other people from Kansas City, and we're going to go to Haiti and spend 72 hours with these kids," Mike says. "She can't wait."

While Mike planned to spend his time looking at sites for a possible medical clinic or vocational school, Beth planned to care for the caregivers, taking them things like mirrors, purses and groceries you can't get in Haiti. "That's her mission, to care for the ladies who care for our kids," Mike says. "She's right down in the trenches. She's really into being the hands and feet of Christ. It's pretty cool to watch her make that transformation." HT

For additional information and helpful Web links related to Mike's journey from success to significance, visit www.halftime.org/thesecondhalf and click on his name.

Answering a rumbling spirit

SAM KIRK

I felt like Sam Kirk was a little frustrated with me for some reason. Not sure why. We were enjoying a really great meal at J. Alexander's in Brentwood, Tenn., surrounded by some of the prettiest horse farms anywhere.

I think in Sam's mind you either do the right thing or you don't. You obey or you don't. You care for others by what you do or you don't. So my gentle questions about his inner motivation to launch Youth About Business were met with curt answers.

I can live with that, because not only do I like Sam, I respect him. His life speaks for itself, and that earns him the respect of almost everyone who meets him, including the person who matters most to him, his wife Cynthia.

After taking the entrepreneurial leap to launch his dream organization serving urban kids with business training, Sam found

Just Be
Teaching Youth to
Exceed Expectation
GAYLORD
OPRYLAND

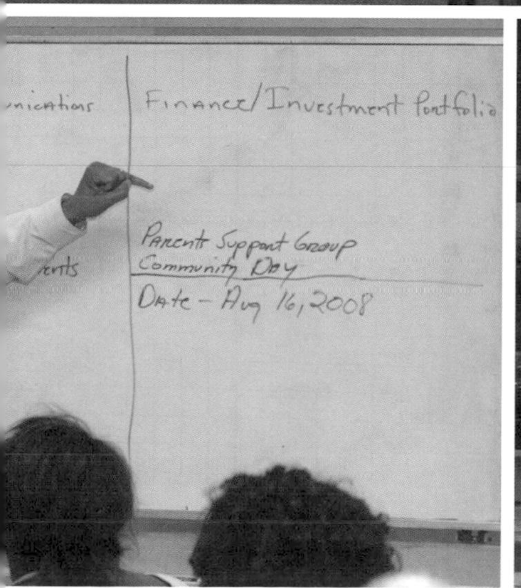
Finance/Investment Portfolio
Parent Support Group
Community Day
Date - Aug 16, 2008

YOUTH ABOUT BUSINESS
TRAINING CENTER

himself from time to time wondering exactly how he and his family would make it. His resolve for the new vision never wavered, but it was as if someone had spilled coffee on the blueprints. Sorting through the stains left him rubbing his temples and looking into the eyes of his best friend for comfort and reassurance.

"God knew who I was marrying, I guess," Sam says with a grin. "He gave me the right wife. She would never get to the place where she said, 'Let's give up.' When I came home a little flustered or frustrated, she was always encouraging. My wife is a very no-nonsense person. Very disciplined. Very disciplined in her walk with the Lord. It's just a blessing. God knew for the work He called me to do that I needed that type of wife."

Sam and Cynthia founded Youth About Business in 1992 on a shared faith and commitment that's been key to its success, even if an occasional coffee stain still finds its way onto the blueprints. "There are just times that it really does require you to have tremendous faith," he says. "... It's truly a faith walk, but it's always rewarding."

Youth About Business isn't so much a faith-based organization, however, as a faith-infused organization. The curriculum is strictly business, but the entire program reflects Sam's passions for modeling his faith and adhering to Biblical principles.

"Our number one value statement is we want to be known by our love – one for another," he says. "I think that's what attracts kids to our program. They know that when they come that there is an organization, a group of people, that genuinely loves and cares about them. Period."

With that love comes a heaping helping of practical instruction.

Through camps and intensive classes, the YAB program teaches business and entrepreneurial skills to students as young as 10 years old. They start with lessons as simple as defining goals and move up to more complex ideas like budgeting, accounting, understanding balance sheets or knowing the difference between a sole proprietorship and an LLC.

The program sets up internships in areas in which the students are gifted and interested, and experts – investment bankers, tax attorneys and the like – guide advanced students through a merger and acquisition simulation. (In fact, if you lead a business you could partner with Sam by providing internships in your area.)

"We're teaching young people how to think, how to have a very high-level business understanding," Sam says.

"Think about it," he adds. "A 16-year-old negotiating a merger. They work 70 hours that week. They'll stay up all night studying. It's really a fun project to watch. They'll negotiate like the CFO of the company, and they really believe they are protecting the company's finances."

The students come mainly from economically depressed neighborhoods in cities such as Nashville (where Sam founded the organization), Chicago, Memphis, Houston and New York. Many have gone

...he began living out what's become his personal philosophy – that real peace in life only comes by losing yourself in service to others.

on to college and careers in real estate or banking or as small business owners.

William, 14, rode the bus across town with his 13-year-old sister so they could attend the program's classes. His mother, a single parent, had no car. He aspired to a career in real estate, and he spent a summer working for a developer to see what it was like.

"So many students grow up in homes like William's," Sam says. "They don't see very much hope, so they look to the drug dealer. They look at their environment, and there are not a lot of very positive role models. But if you start exposing this kid, and you connect him to these very successful people, I think long term that's where we're going to impact them the most, because they're going to start dreaming again about the potential for their own lives."

They graduate 98 percent of their participants. In underserved communities, fewer than 60 percent of the students even graduate from high school. "To me," Sam says, "I think it's not that children can't learn, but if you create a vision, if a child knows you are concerned about them learning, that you are concerned about their dreams and goals, I think that they'll perform."

The program gives students the knowledge and the skills to live out the dream, not just so that they can earn a living but also so that they can earn a living the right way. Sam was tired of "losing our children" but he also knew that financial success has its own trappings. So he built a program based on values such as integrity, honesty and service to others.

Those are the values that guided Sam's successful 17-year business career. He enjoyed his work. He and Cynthia were able to travel and afford what he modestly terms a "decent" lifestyle. And while he already was enjoying financial success, significant pay hikes were just around the corner if he continued down the corporate track.

Then things changed – in his heart.

"I refer to it as a rumbling in your spirit, because that's when God begins to, in His way, communicate with you that He wants you to do the work that He calls you to do," Sam says. "And I really believe firmly that every person is created purposefully, with a mission, with a goal. That's why Jesus Himself, His last statement was 'It is finished' because He had a specific work that God had for Him to do. When God begins to rumble in your spirit, you can't get away from it."

Sam took a six-week sabbatical in St. Croix to think things over. And then he began living out what's become his personal philosophy – that real peace in life only comes by losing yourself in service to others.

"You can have all the resources in the world, but you won't ever get fully at peace until you lose yourself," he says. "...We have a whole lot less resources in our lives right now, but we're happier than we've ever been. I tell my wife I personally am happier now than I've ever been. I have a peace in my life that I really appreciate."

After these kids head off to college they often come to the realization of just how much of a blessing Sam and his team have been to them. Perhaps one boy summed it up last Christmas when he sent a card just to say, "Mr. Kirk, I don't think you have any idea how you've impacted the lives of young people." I think he's right Sam. HT

For additional information and helpful Web links related to Sam's journey from success to significance, visit www.halftime.org/thesecondhalf and click on his name.

A simple idea

TRIPP JOHNSTON

The journey from pursuing success to pursuing significance is a heart journey more than anything, and it doesn't happen overnight.

For Tripp Johnston, it began as he was exposed to some of the pain and suffering in Charlotte, N.C. – the city he and I both call home. Charlotte is healthy and thriving, a beautiful fast-growing city covered by a canopy of tall green trees. From the vantage points of our nice neighborhoods, things can look pretty nice. So what I love about Tripp's very first steps into the second half is that they were small – he just opened his heart and eyes to see the needs that were just blocks away from his high-rise bank tower.

Tripp went to the University of North Carolina as a prestigious Morehead Scholar, married Alison (his high school sweetheart) shortly after graduation, began his career with one of the big accounting firms, and scored the highest in the country on the CPA exam that first year out of college. After earning an MBA from Harvard, he transitioned into investment banking, where he quickly became known as a mergers and acquisitions specialist. And he and Alison had three beautiful children along the way.

But he kept coming back to an unsettling question – "What's the passion of my life or the song in my heart?" – and he didn't

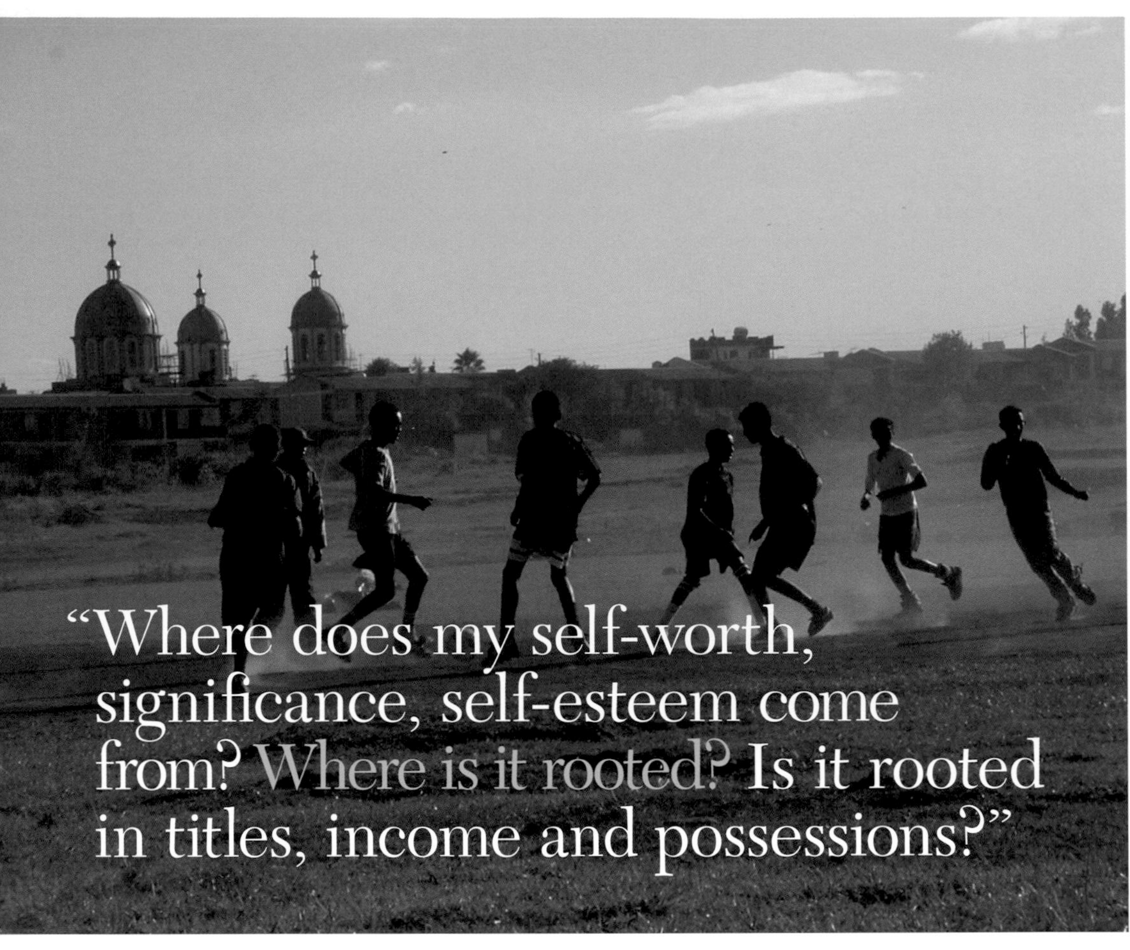

"Where does my self-worth, significance, self-esteem come from? Where is it rooted? Is it rooted in titles, income and possessions?"

like the answer. "It was all about me and building a name for myself and being a successful businessman, climbing the ladder, making money and all those things so many of us aspire to. ... God was only getting the leftovers in my life, and there was very little left over given the demands of my family and my career."

So they made an interesting move by switching to a very different type of church, "a multi-racial church. We had always gone to wealthy suburban churches." This new setting shook things up a little, because it was "a very diverse church where there were people from every socio-economic background." As their comfort level grew around people who were different from them, so did their desire to be around those people and to serve the ones who were in greatest need.

The investment banker went through a period where he learned what it meant to become a different kind of investor – both to view his corporate setting as a platform from which to invest in people's lives and in the urban setting as a place to invest in meeting the needs of the poor.

While he loved investment banking, this new arena was bringing significant joy, as well, and it was just difficult to find the time to invest in both.

"This happened over the course of a couple of years, this growing tension and sense that God was beginning to change my heart, really, and give me different desires," he says. "More of the joy of my heart was being involved in ministry ... investment banking was less interesting to me. There was a growing conflict. It was scary for sure."

More and more of the compelling opportunities that came Tripp and Alison's way conflicted with the demands of his work schedule. And as he wrestled with that conflict, he began to feel that investment banking – the career that so fit his skills, passions and gifts – interested him less and less.

So at age 39, Tripp resigned his position as chief operating officer of First Union Bank (now Wachovia Corp.) Capital Markets Group and asked the big question: What next? They decided to take six months off so that they didn't rush into something, and that in itself was an important learning time.

"I had to learn that it was OK to be seen in the carpool picking up my kids at 3 in the afternoon," Tripp chuckles. From my own Halftime experience that's part of the detox process; it's part of reshaping our identities. "Oh, for sure," Tripp says. "It's true. You feel like you're worried that somebody is going to see you during working hours not in your office. You're right, just kind of going through that detox of evaluating. Where does my self-worth, significance, self-esteem come from? Where is it rooted? Is it rooted in titles, income and possessions?"

During that period, a friend, Brian Davidson, asked him to join him on a two-week trip to Ethiopia. What he thought would be "a very enriching two week experience" changed him at the core. Two data-specific points captivated his thinking:

First, the demographics of the country: 60 percent of the population are under 25 and live in poverty with little hope.

Second, the instant transformation that occurs among the youth when you simply roll a soccer ball out on the ground and invite them to play.

His teammates wondered why he was almost silent on the trip home from Africa. Tripp's mind was busy around these two compelling facts and how they converge into a simple and scalable ministry model: "If you roll out a soccer ball in these developing countries, you are overrun with

young people who have very little to do but are looking to belong to something or looking for adult mentors. And they will come play sports, so it's just an easy platform to develop relationships."

From his banking background, Tripp knows that even a simple scalable idea has to have an organizational platform and distribution for it to really make an impact. So he and Brian launched Sports Friends by joining forces with SIM, an international organization with thousands of staff and partners around the world. It provided an instant, proven platform and infrastructure that would have taken years to build on their own. For SIM, Sports Friends provided a niche service that would complement their other work. It was a win/win.

I told Tripp that I often see folks launch into their second half by creating their own organizations, and they burn a lot of calories just ramping up the organizational structure, accounting and fundraising. "You chose to build on the backbone of an existing 100-year-old organization that has all that stuff in place," I observed. "Was that intentional?"

"I think too often," Tripp says, "people do their own thing, and they don't come together with the economies of scale and coordinated strategies. So from the get-go we asked who would value this ministry strategy, who would have a lot to give us, and who needs this?"

Like any well-run organization, SIM wanted to see a working model before agreeing to roll it out. So Tripp and his family did what he once would have considered unthinkable: They moved to Ethiopia for three years. Even more unthinkable, they moved at the start of their oldest daughter's senior year of high school. And to their great relief, she enthusiastically embraced the idea.

Not only did they successfully launch the ministry, but it strengthened their family. Their daughter, for instance, prayed for "just one friend" on her first day at the international high school, and she made just one friend that day. She later made more, of course, but the one friend she met that day is now her husband!

Alison, meanwhile, used her training as a nurse to get involved in ministering to AIDs patients, a gut-wrenching, heart-tugging ordeal in which she made friend after friend only to watch them die. But Alison found deep satisfaction in helping them die with hope and peace.

Looking back on the series of risks and sacrifices they have taken as a family, Tripp says, "To see Alison coming alive in that way was one of the greatest blessings in this whole experience."

Tripp and Alison returned from Africa a few years ago and now they're excited to see what's in store for them as they head to Asia to launch Sports Friends there.

"We put Christian mentors into the lives of young people who are in desperate need. The whole focus of Sports Friends is to train, equip and mobilize Christians in Africa, Asia and South America to use sports as a platform to build quality relationships with young people. And through those young people and their families, we have the opportunity to be a life influencer, to draw them closer to God, and we have the chance to show them who Christ is, to love them, mentor and disciple them … to just be relevant in their lives and a mentor as they deal with lots of life issues, whether it's HIV/AIDS, poverty, civil war. We use sports just as a platform for doing that." HT

For additional information and helpful Web links related to Tripp's journey from success to significance, visit www.halftime.org/thesecondhalf and click on his name.

Building into others

KEMMONS WILSON

Almost every time I fly into Memphis, Tenn., Kemmons Wilson graciously picks me up at the airport and we drive to the Rendezvous, a restaurant off a downtown alley, for some of the best dry ribs this side of heaven.

We've been doing this for almost a decade, and in those years I have asked him just about every imaginable question about life – from parenting to business to his remarkable relationship with his wife, Norma. Frankly, I admire Kem, and I think you will too.

Kemmon's involvement in faith-based nonprofits didn't start with a midlife awakening, and in my view that's even healthier than a classic Halftime transition. "I really haven't changed anything I've been doing for the past 40 years," he says. But now he's in a position to do more of what he's always done. It also includes encouraging Norma's involvement in a broader range of projects now that their children are adults.

"I see her coming into her own," he says. "I see her branching out."

Norma spent her first half raising the couple's five children. And while she considers "mothering" a lifelong calling, it's no longer a full-time job.

"I'm still searching for where God wants me to be," she says. "I'm still very content being at home, and I'm content helping with my grandchildren, but I know that there is so much more because I see it in Kem."

Kem, whose father founded the Holiday Inn hotel chain, is a principal and leader of the Kemmons Wilson Companies, which has followed in the entrepreneurial footsteps of his father by operating businesses within the hospitality, financial services, real estate, aviation and insurance industries. More important than continuing his father's business legacy, however, is continuing the legacy of community involvement.

"He loves his business, and he has not stopped working," Norma says. "But when he volunteers … he's not one to be on a board just to be on a board. He really wants to live with significance. So he's still very involved with his business, but he does have his heart in service."

Keeping one foot in business and one foot in service isn't new to Kem, who has helped launch around 20 faith-based nonprofits. But with each passing year he's grown more focused in his approach. He's repeatedly turned down offers to serve on his social club's board, arts boards and even his church's elder board, all because he's convinced his "sweet spot" involves building into emerging leaders who will in turn transform their city.

"I've always enjoyed meeting with some guy who was trying to start a ministry who really had the heart for it but just didn't have the business acumen to get it going," Kem says. "I just felt those are some of my gifts and some of my talents. That's really what's excited me, more of an entrepreneurial approach."

There's a question Kem likes to ask – of himself, of his wife and of others: What will you do with your invitation from God? "Everybody's got one," he says. "And when you can present that to someone and they get it – when you ask questions like, 'Are you willing to let God use you?' and they come to the conclusion that they are – that's exciting."

Kem asked such questions to Kennon Vaughan, a talented young friend of one of Kem's sons. Kem helped Vaughan start DownLine, a discipleship ministry based in Memphis, after Vaughan responded to a simple question: "What is your dream and how can I help you?"

The program fits nicely with Kem's

passion for discipleship and mentoring, but unexpectedly also provided a training ground for Norma to explore her second-half options.

Kem says, "She is literally being trained and equipped through DownLine. I don't know where that's going to lead, but I'm excited. This could be a new sort of springboard for her."

The transition into this newest season of life isn't easy for Norma or for other women who spent their first halves raising a family, Kem says, because the culture often doesn't appreciate or esteem the virtues of stay-at-home mothers.

"In some ways it's been a struggle for her," Kem says, "and I guess this would be a question for a lot of dedicated homemakers. Unless they are just exuding self-confidence, they can have the opinion that, 'Well that's what I've done for the last 30 years. I don't know if I can do anything else.'"

With Kem's encouragement, Norma's taken her place on boards of ministries she cares about and is mentoring young moms as she searches for that "sweet spot" where a person's gifts and talents align with a particular project or organization.

Identifying where to spend one's time and energy is an ongoing adventure. Norma, still finds contentment in her roles as a wife, mother and grandmother. She was greatly influenced by the book *The Power of a Praying Wife*. So whether she's serving on a board of directors, mentoring young mothers or praying for her husband's needs, Norma is finding ways to stretch her faith and impact her world.

"I don't have the drive that Kem has," she says. "I see in him [that] it's not a duty, he doesn't feel like it's a responsibility he has to do, he doesn't feel like it's something he knows he should do. It's something his heart wants to do, and I just pray that I will have that heart to really find something that I could be so focused on."

For me, the core message of Kem's life boils down to how he treats the folks that serve us ribs at Rendezvous Restaurant – he knows them, their names, their stories. He's building into their lives. They're his friends and he cares about them. After all, some of them have been waiting tables there for more than 40 years.

What I've learned from Kem is that you build a life of significance from the inside out starting at home, building into the lives of others – not real flashy, just real. HT

For additional information and helpful Web links related to Kemmon's journey from success to significance, visit www.halftime.org/thesecondhalf and click on his name.

HOME
GUEST
07:00
14
3
55
25
23
2

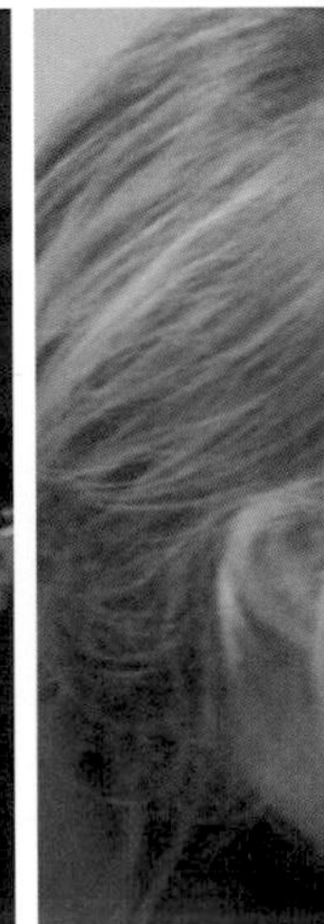

All about the numbers

GIB VESTAL

Gib Vestal is a numbers man. As a former managing director with Morgan Keegan in Memphis, Tenn., he knows all about investing in startup ventures and reaping big gains.

But he never imagined the even more fulfilling gains he would experience by merging his skills with those of others in a startup venture called Memphis Athletic Ministries (MAM). The results are direct and measurable – more than 13,000 kids a year are impacted, and the transformation in their lives is visible.

Gib knows the children impacted by MAM's programs are more balanced in their approach to racial issues, less likely to commit crimes, more likely to enjoy academic success and more likely to contribute positively to the Memphis community. So while just one child is important, numbers do matter.

Getting to the numbers that matter to Gib, however, wasn't a quick, easy journey. He wrestled with the decision for years until, ultimately, he literally had no choice.

Gib came to one of our very first Halftime events in Memphis, sponsored by Kem Wilson (see the previous story, page 90–93).

Excitement is one thing, but what Gib wants is numbers – numbers of parents who report that they see a difference in their child's life, education and attitude.

"The Halftime Summit crystallized my thinking," says Gib, "and made me feel more confident that MAM was the right thing to do. It represented the perfect application of a lot of talents that I had cultivated over my work career." Still, Gib balked at making a move. Looking back, it's easier for him to see how he was held captive by the "golden handcuffs" of his career.

But not for long. "I went into work one day, and a 15-year colleague came in and said, 'Gib, I've got bad news: The company is cutting staff and you're one of them.'"

Gib's response? "That's fantastic!"

"It was God's answer to my procrastination," Gib tells me with hindsight. "One day I was hanging on and the next day Morgan Keegan was paying me to leave. God was saying, 'Go ahead, Gib, take that step. I've got something better for you.'"

During his last few years at Morgan Keegan, Gib and his wife, Mimi, had regularly discussed the possibility of his leaving. "We had talked about it," he says, "kicked around everything from teaching school to starting my own business. So she was in that process the whole time. It wasn't something that just occurred and I sprung it on her one day."

Sports had long been Gib's passion. He'd been involved for years in coaching youth teams and had even helped start a basketball league. An assessment exercise had pointed to Christian sports administration as a best fit for him. So even before he heard about MAM he was thinking about ways he might combine his skills and experiences with a nonprofit that used sports as a platform for things like building character and promoting racial reconciliation.

"I went out and began to network with numerous inner-city ministries here in Memphis," Gib says. He invited Larry Lloyd, a man who helped launch many of those ministries, to lunch. "During that working lunch Larry told me about a ministry that was still an idea, but not a reality, and that was Memphis Athletic Ministries. It coincided perfectly with the desires I had for doing something."

So in 2001, shortly after Morgan Keegan freed him of his golden handcuffs, Gib became president of MAM, which had incorporated by that time but wasn't doing much more than a few local sports clinics. Now kids participate in more than 3,000 sporting events a year through MAM programs, not to mention after school programs and service projects.

Looking around from within Gib's office, it's easy to get a sense of this new world he lives in. Through a window in the office I see hundreds of rambunctious kids playing games and running off steam after school in the multi-gym facility. By contrast, Gib is calm and measured. His mind methodically works through ideas to improve the systems and processes, ways to enable the staff and coaches to touch these kids even more deeply. But when I stand around in the gym, or near the soccer field, or at the golf course they've just been given by the city and when I see those little kids' faces light up when their coach knows their names or because they sink a shot, I get a small sense of what has captivated Gib's heart.

Excitement is one thing, but what Gib wants is numbers – numbers of parents who report that they see a difference in their child's life, education and attitude. In fact, Gib surveys each parent, so he knows that "94 percent of parents reported a 'positive difference' in their child" as a result of MAM participation.

MAM staff, coaches and officials are at every activity and are trained to reinforce behavior standards by integrating core values, encouraging and affirming the kids, building character and being role models. They often travel with the teams outside their neighborhoods, giving them exposure they might not otherwise have.

The heart of the organization is to model the Christian faith throughout a diverse and racially divided city. By partnering with more than 100 other organizations, MAM creates opportunities for meaningful interaction and relationships between kids and parents of different races and economic backgrounds.

"Through God's empowerment, we're creating a culture that changes the lives of kids and builds racial bridges in the community," Gib said. "I love those results." HT

For additional information and helpful Web links related to Gib's journey from success to significance, visit www.halftime.org/thesecondhalf and click on his name.

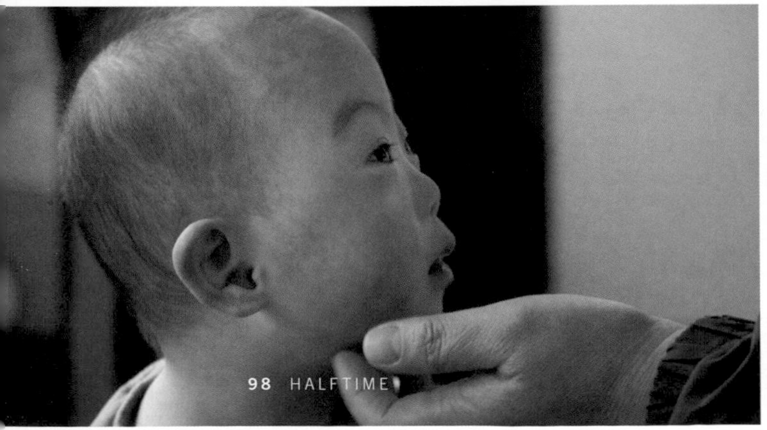

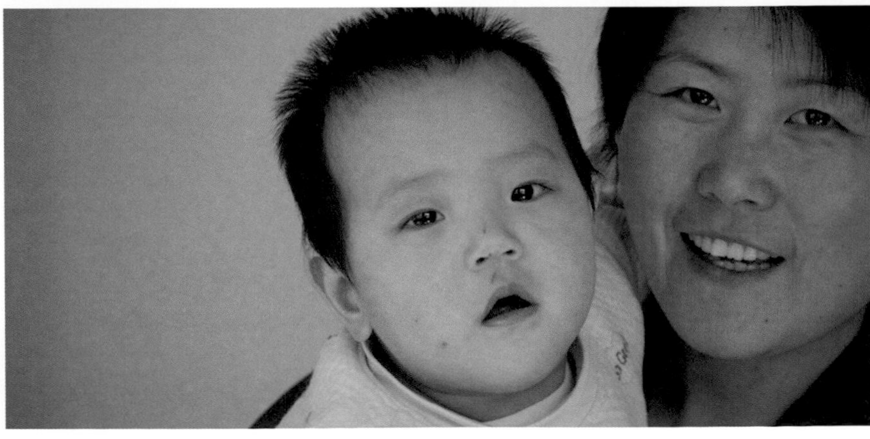

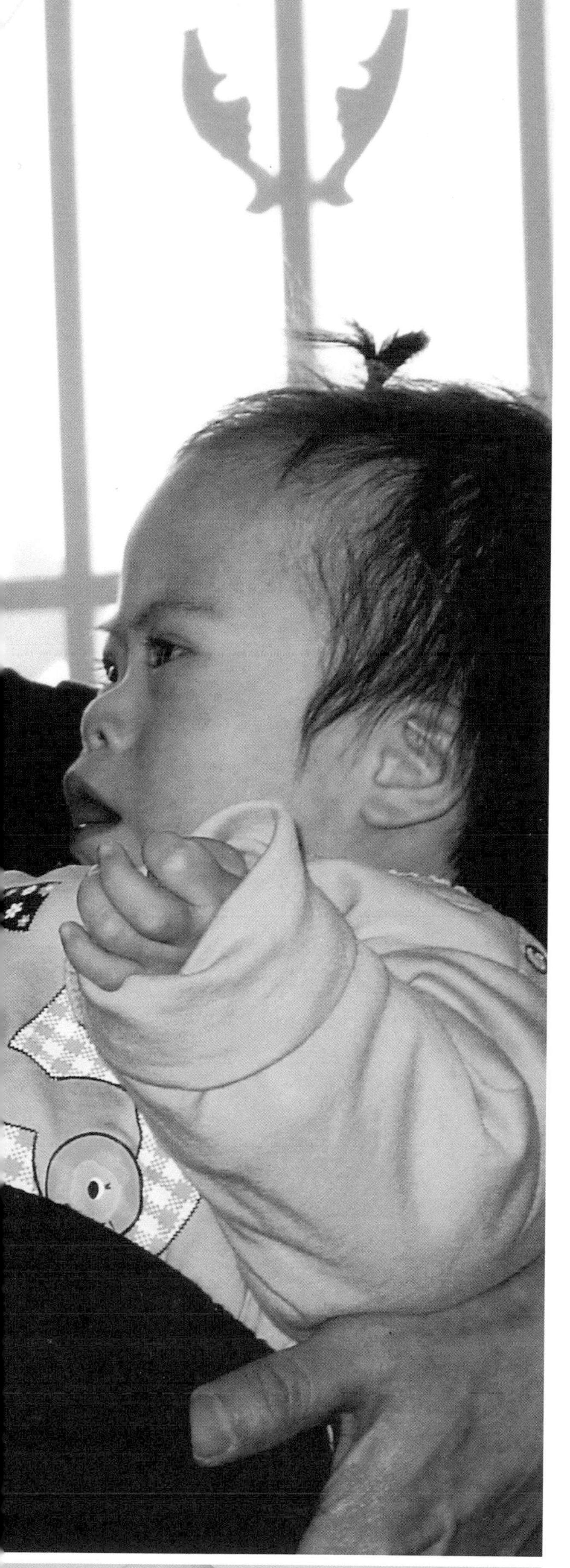

Finding his priority

KEN YEUNG

Kenneth Yeung introduced himself to a small group of Asian American business leaders by saying, "I'm Kenneth, I'm 57, and I am a tea guy. I am married and we have one daughter, and I am passionate about orphans."

I was intrigued. I wanted to know what he meant by "a tea guy" and what he did for orphans. As the day progressed, I explored what he meant and how those two things had shaped his past, while he learned how they would shape his future.

Kenneth had a secret assumption when he arrived at the beautiful hotel part way up the mountain in Vail, Colo. I was leading the small group of peers on a day-long exploration of "what to do with the second half of life." He assumed he was destined to someday sell his company, go to seminary and become a minister. What he discovered was something radically different,

but not at all radically different from who Kenneth is at the core.

A picture can indeed speak a thousand words, but for Kenneth, it was the words on a poster featuring the photo of a young Chinese girl that spoke to his very soul: "Priority – A hundred years from now it will not matter what my bank account was, the sort of house I lived in, or the kind of car I drove. But the world may be different because I was important in the life of a child."

A native of the Shantou, Guangdong province of China, Kenneth understands more than most the meaning behind that message. Political oppression forced his mother to send him to live with relatives in Hong Kong, where he struggled with language and cultural differences, as well as heart-wrenching homesickness. What 11-year-old wouldn't? But sensing the hole in his heart and the voids in his life skills, caring neighbors reached out to boost him over the language hurdle and to bridge the gap of his parentless world.

"I learned early on in life that it is so important for someone to give you a helping hand if you don't have help from a family member," says Kenneth.

Several years later, an equally caring teacher started Kenneth on a spiritual journey. As he matured in his faith, one thing was certain: He wanted to help others as his way of giving back. He prayerfully contemplated a career in ministry or social work. "But God had higher plans for my life," he says. "He led me to San Francisco, not into social work, but into business – and He expanded my influence far beyond what I could have ever imagined."

That business – a highly successful tea company – operates with an unwritten contract with God. "When I started the business," he says, "I told my Lord that I wanted to serve Him. 'This is your business. I am just your steward to manage it for you.' That unwritten contract guides how I treat my employees – and how I use the funds the business generates."

The substantial profits his company generates are invested in meeting the deepest needs of others, Kenneth says, not his own comfort or material gain. He first began by using profits to help hundreds of American families adopt Chinese children when no agency in America knew how to go about it. In 1993, Kenneth and his wife also adopted a Chinese baby, Melissa Joy, who every day of her life puts her fingerprints on the message of the poster that had so captivated her father's heart.

When I asked Kenneth about what he does with orphans, his eyes lit up and he simply said, "Would you like to see my photos? We built an orphanage in China." He reached down and pulled out a dog-eared little photo album and began to show me the most compelling shots of an orphanage for 100 little children, all of them disabled. Page 7 was a photo of him holding a little girl, and I was captivated by the smile on his face. "Who is this little girl," I asked, "and why are you smiling like that?" He told me her name and said, "I just paid to have her heart repaired. Without that, she would have been disposable."

Now that took my breath away.

In China, where baby girls are often abandoned, the opportunity to make a difference in the life of a child is great – so great that in 1995 Kenneth began an endeavor that took eight years to bring to fruition.

Considered an embarrassment to their families, the mentally and physically handicapped of China often are thrown into garbage bins. Burdened to make a home for these unwanted children, Kenneth

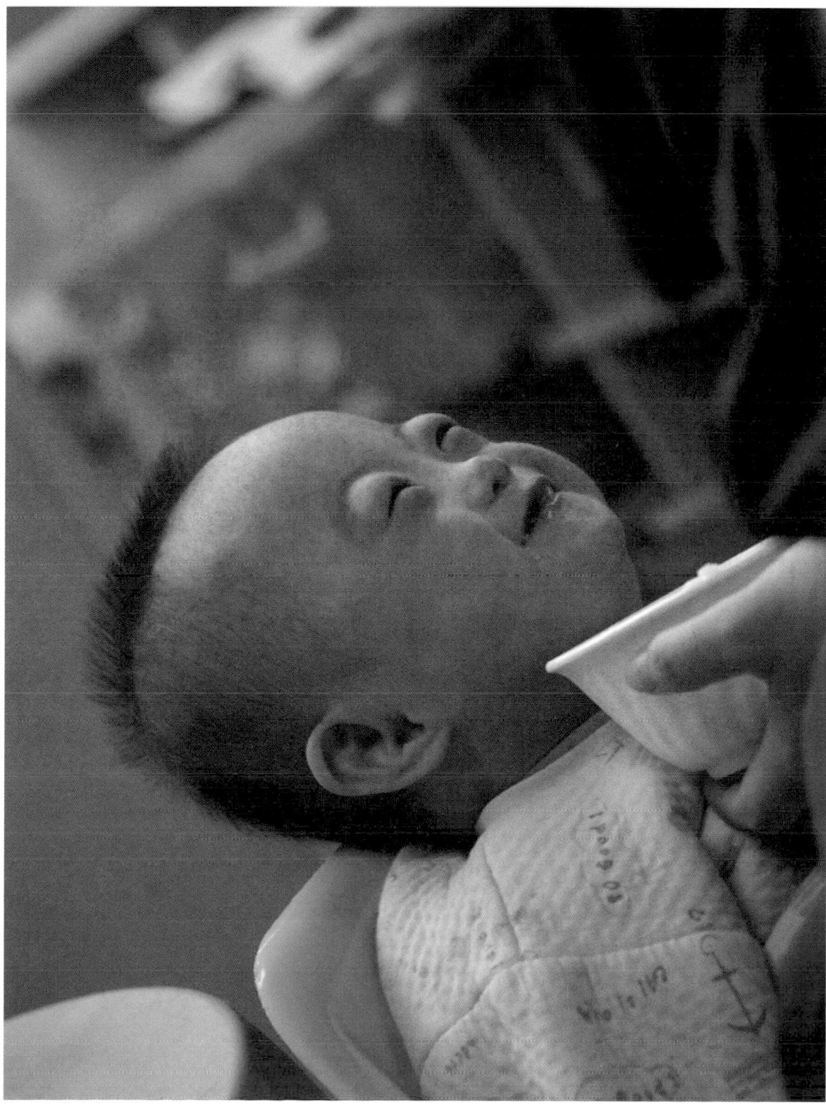

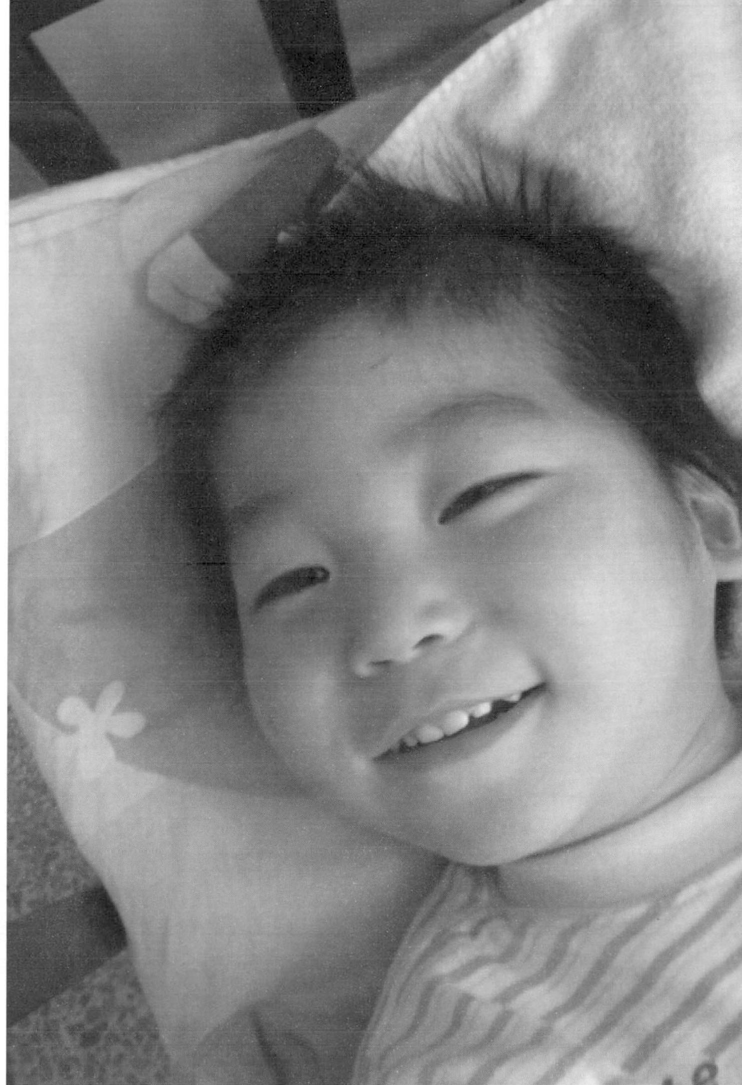

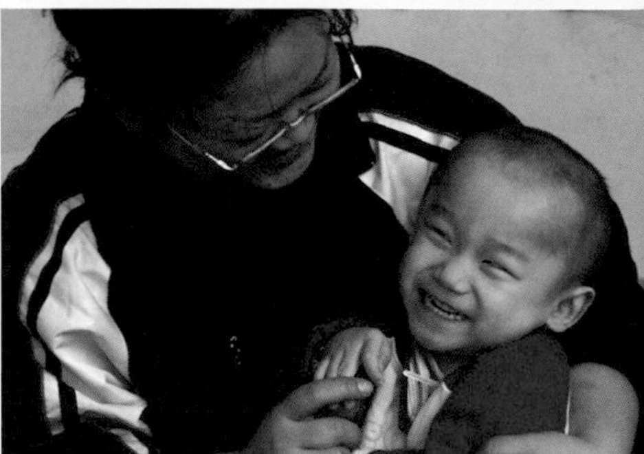

"But the world may be different because I was important in the life of a child."

negotiated patiently with the Chinese government. In November 2003, the Prince of Peace Children's Home (POPCH), located in the Wuqing district of Tianjin, opened its doors. Funded by the Prince of Peace Foundation and World Vision International as a joint venture with the Civil Affairs Bureau of Wuqing, the facility accommodates 100 mentally and physically handicapped children under age 6 and provides rehabilitation services to other disabled children in the province.

The home set a miraculous precedent in China: For the first time in history, the government had allowed a foreign organization to build, staff and manage an orphanage. Today, highly trained staff and caring volunteers lovingly embrace children once viewed as society's trash – and they teach others to do the same.

"I told the Chinese officials that we would not only build and manage the orphanage, but we would also set up a training center to help caretakers from other orphanages in China," Kenneth says. "What the Chinese government really needs is to see a model that an overseas Christian organization can come in and build this type of thing with love and care. I told the officials that God has loved us, and we want to share our love with the children in China. They accepted that. They even allowed us to engrave a Bible verse on the cornerstone of the building."

At lunch during our time in Colorado, I asked Kenneth if he left any other passions behind during his first-half pursuit of success. After just a few seconds he looked me straight in the eyes and said, "Well, yes, there is. I am very good at photography. I love photography, but about 15 years ago I gave it up because my business was growing and my family was busy."

The biggest thrill for me at the end of that day was to sit back and listen as Kenneth shared with his peers a plan for his second half of life. "I came to this day thinking I would sell my business and go to seminary and go into ministry," he said, "But I'm a tea guy – this is what I do and I am good at it and I make a lot of money doing it. So instead, I am going to hire someone to take some of my responsibilities in my company, and I will go and capture the most compelling photos of disabled orphans in China to challenge others to help fund orphanages for these children – we'll even print them on the back of the tea packages we sell around the world. And I will go and ensure they are run well."

And that is what he is doing. In fact, these are his photographs and they represent the convergence of his passions: Tea company profits, compelling photographs and disabled orphans who know everyday that someone loves them dearly. He recently won a prestigious award by the Chinese government for outstanding charitable organizations – the first non-Chinese citizen to receive the award.

Kenneth put it this way: "If I can help change the fate of a needy child, I'd rather do that than have all the world's luxury." HT

For additional information and helpful Web links related to Kenneth's journey from success to significance, visit www.halftime.org/thesecondhalf and click on his name.

(This is a revised version of a chapter in Unlimited Partnership, *a book I co-authored with Bill Wellons. It's used by permission from B & H Publishing 2007.)*

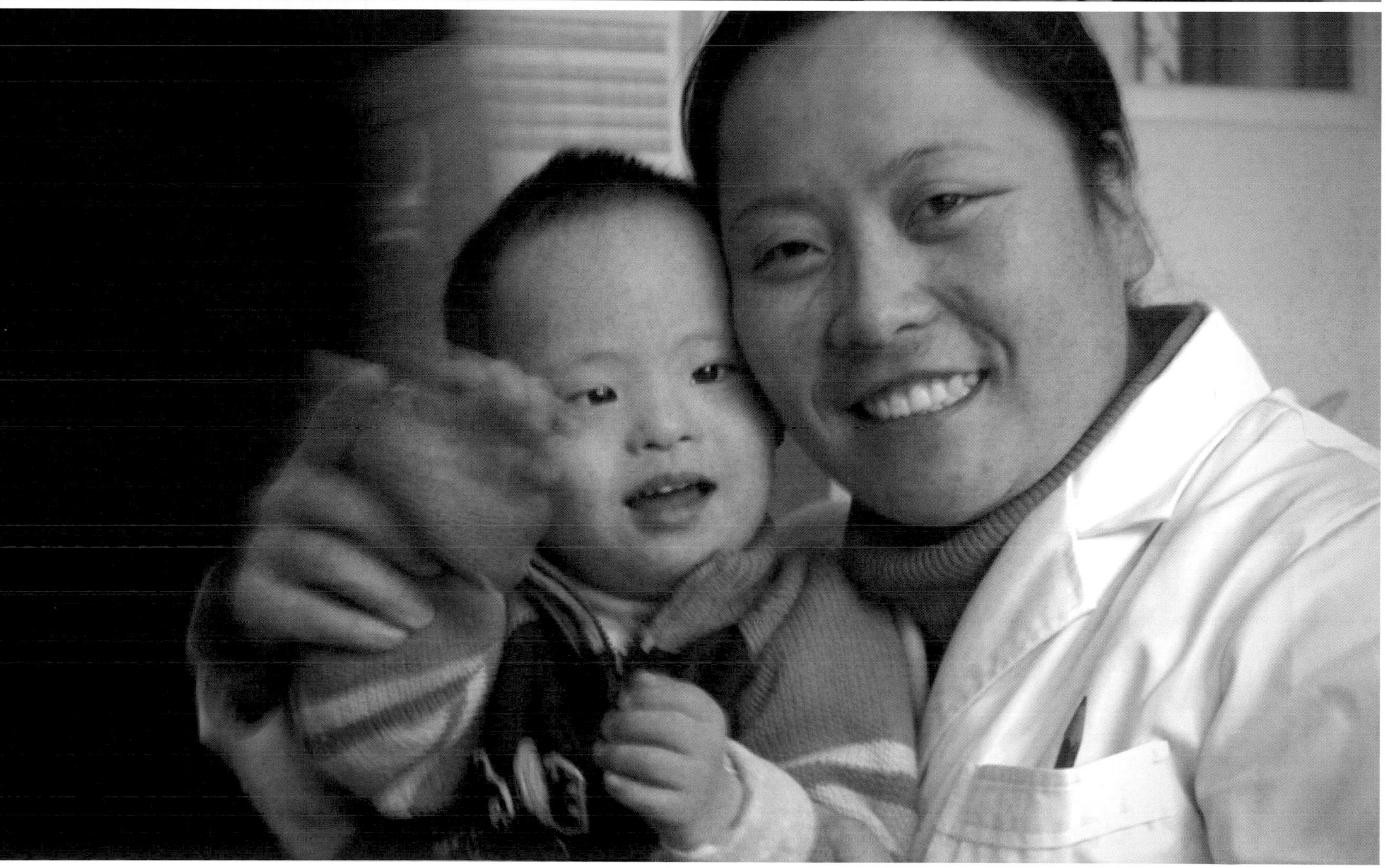

Living out significance

STEVE GRISIM

My speaking engagement in Scottsdale, Ariz., ended on a picture-perfect 70-degree day, and I walked out into the sunshine with a spring in my step.

My next destination: The bone-chilling, breath-freezing, 30-below-zero cold of Winnipeg, Canada.

With a winter coat but no hat, I was somewhat unprepared for the 100-degree plunge in temperature as Steve Grisim and I crunched through the snow on the way to his car in the airport parking lot. But what stung worse than the bitter wind in my face was the sense of hopelessness I soon saw around Winnipeg, particularly among the sizable aboriginal community.

It first hit me when we stopped to buy a jumbo marker for my flip chart illustrations and I realized that you couldn't buy such markers off the shelves in downtown Winnipeg. So many people sniff them to get high that stores keep them in a secure place well behind the customer service counters.

Negative-30-degree temperatures are enough to depress anyone, I thought, but what kind of pain must a person feel to

want to get high by sniffing a jumbo marker? And what kind of culture has so many people experiencing that much soul pain that they have to hide the markers? And I especially wanted to know what motivated Steve to use his corporate leadership skills to enable thousands of ordinary members of Springs Church to get involved in tackling these tough issues.

As we arrived at the church, I begin to learn what's happening deep in Steve's heart. He doesn't know all of the 10,000-plus people who call this their church home, and many of them don't even know what he looks like. And he's fine with that. He's most happy when the systems and processes, the staff and the leadership structure he is developing, are firing on all cylinders and changing people's lives. There's nothing more rewarding for him than mobilizing resources to address drug addictions or to see thousands of police officers and their spouses coming to learn how to grow a healthy marriage and deal with the stress in a way that will lead to peaceful homes. That's a win in his book.

But Steve's behind-the-scenes service has a deeper agenda: To see people finding more joy in life by following their calling, giving of themselves to meet the deepest needs of others rather than just settling for a life of comfort and security.

Steve knows that many of his peers are wrapping up their first-half careers with an early retirement and a goal of moving somewhere like sunny Scottsdale – somewhere warm, somewhere relaxing, somewhere … else. But he fears they might be missing out on something much more rewarding.

If Steve had blinked, he might have missed out on it himself. But his friendship with Springs Church Senior Pastor Leon Fontaine led to an unexpected change in course for Steve's second half. As an executive for a large furniture manufacturer, Steve thought he and Leon had little in common when it came to work. But the more they met for coffee or lunch, the more they discovered the challenges of their respective careers weren't that different.

"We just kind of developed a friendship," Steve says. "We both had a real love of leadership – reading, studying and learning everything we could about leadership."

Still, it took Steve by surprise when Leon suggested he leave his fast-track career for a staff position as executive pastor.

"I thought he was just joking," Steve says. "I couldn't see the correlation at all between the skills in the business community and in ministry or church."

"In hindsight," he says, "God had a plan, and I didn't."

Steve's experiences setting up new divisions and operations for Palliser Furniture were "completely applicable" when it came to helping the church grow. The lessons he learned during a brief stint in the human resources division prepared him for dealing with staff issues at the church. He's found common ground between mentoring junior executives and mentoring ministry staff. And his experience with operations has helped him implement things that free up Leon to be the organization's visionary leader rather than getting bogged down in organizational details.

As much as anything, he says, he's putting the relationship skills required of any successful businessman to work in a ministry environment.

“The thing is, this is everybody’s heart’s desire. They may not be able to articulate it. They want to be part of something meaningful. Everybody wants to know that their life is making a difference – and not just a small difference because I gave $30 and now somebody in Africa can eat this week. They want to know that they themselves are impacting other lives.”

“You can’t be successful in the business community without being able to communicate with people at all different levels,” he says. “The ability in business to see the bigger picture, to see how things affect other things – it’s a huge part of what being in ministry is about.”

The understandable temptation we face as successful marketplace leaders is to spend our time driving toward a goal of retiring somewhere comfortable rather than a goal of living out our calling. Steve told me he is neck-deep in learning that while that approach might lead to a comfortable second half, for him it falls short of what our second-half adventures can be – and it inadvertently sends the wrong message to our children. It’s as if we’re engaged in serving others and giving of ourselves up until retirement. Then we coast.

“In our community, I’ve seen a lot of children who have really cooled their Christian walk because they’re looking at their parents and it looks like Christianity is a phase you go through in your life,” Steve says. “It’s not something you live for the rest of your life.”

That’s why Steve has developed such a passion for connecting business leaders with serving opportunities that burn on the fuel of their gifts and passions, not just their bank accounts.

“The thing is, this is everybody’s heart’s desire,” he says. “They may not be able to articulate it. They want to be part of something meaningful. Everybody wants to know that their life is making a difference – and not just a small difference because I gave $30 and now somebody in Africa can eat this week. They want to know that they themselves are impacting other lives. It’s tangible. They can see it. They’re a part of it. There’s an excitement in being a part of that.

“I think it’s a huge witness to the next generation that I’m not just talking about my relationship with Christ being important but that I’m going to live it my entire life.”

For Steve, living it out meant leaving the corporate world, downsizing his family’s lifestyle and not dodging the harsh winters to go pick up shells on the beach for the next 30 years. But for many of us, it will look different. Perhaps just rethinking our current marketplace role or a dual role in the two worlds or transitioning into some other full-time role that isn’t connected to a church but that focuses on changing lives. I sure hope you get the sense, as I do, that part of the adventure is figuring that out.

“Just living in North America, we’re successful,” Steve says. “We’re not truly significant until we realize there’s a reason we’re here. It’s way beyond ourselves. Once you figure that out and start putting the pieces together, yes, it’s a journey, but it really is an exciting journey.” HT

For additional information and helpful Web links related to Steve’s journey from success to significance, visit www.halftime.org/thesecondhalf and click on his name.

RESOURCE LINK

If you would like help in partnering more effectively with your church or a ministry you care about, check out the book Unlimited Partnership. *This unique flip book, written with one side for pastors and the other side for marketplace leaders, paves the way for you to follow in Steve Grisim’s footsteps.*

A portfolio of compassion

DR. COLETTE COZEAN

Dr. Colette Cozean is building a portfolio of passions into her second half. One big, audacious goal is to help establish quality health-care centers within a one- or two-day walk for everyone in Kenya.

I have to admit I had no idea so many Kenyans lived outside the reach of basic care. She patiently explained to me that in many areas "you can walk for two weeks and not get to the closest hospital." Her partnerships are bringing hope to orphans and medical care to some of the country's most remote areas. For her day job, she's a seasoned medical-device inventor and successful entrepreneur. She's also a wife and mother.

And, yet, she's not in a rush.

Colette's calm reflects a sense of focus and calling. She slowly but passionately talks about this unique portfolio of roles, never rushing from one point to the next or coming across as if she's already thinking about the next big thing, even if somewhere in her mind she probably is.

Colette regularly wakes up with detailed diagrams for complex medical devices floating around in her head. So she gathers her team at the office and they go to work filling in the blanks and turning ideas into new products. She's a risk-taking visionary with a Ph.D. in biomedical engineering. She also left school one semester shy of a medical degree. (As she told *BusinessWeek* for a 1997 article detailing the success of her medical-laser startup, Premier Laser Systems, "I was only going to medical school to learn more for my work as an engineer.")

While still in college, Colette developed a device that stimulates degenerating muscles. In the 1980s she helped develop the "peristaltic pump" used on IV units and arthroscopy equipment for knee surgeries. Premier Laser Systems took flight and received national accolades by getting FDA approval for a laser that cuts teeth without pain.

Colette built this career while raising her two children with her husband and childhood sweetheart, Kim, who teaches math and computer science and, as she puts it, "is as opposite from me as you can imagine." While Colette craves adventure and risk, he prefers comfort and stability. But they have built their family on common beliefs and values, and they've learned how to share each other's successes and how to know when to do things together and when to do things apart.

Family is the cornerstone of Colette's portfolio, the compassionate wife and mother who cares deeply about relationships. That's why she so intentionally developed a leadership team she can trust while she moves so fluidly between the worlds of business, ministry and family.

It's impossible to miss, in fact, that her giftedness in academics, medicine, engineering and business never take her far from her deepest passions – her love for others, especially children (her own and others) and her "childlike" faith in God.

You hear it in her voice when she talks about taking her son on trips with her to Kenya or about the joy she found while working from home and caring for her daughter as she recovered from and learned to live with the effects of a near-fatal case of rheumatic fever. And you hear it when she talks about the orphans in Kenya.

"My passion has always been kids," she says.

That's why she was so excited about a mission trip she took a few years ago with some members of her church. The plan was to spend three weeks working with children in an orphanage, but Colette couldn't escape her background in medicine and her reputation for problem-solving. They'd only been there a few days when the president of Kenya asked if their group could help evaluate ways to improve the health-care system in a country ripe with tribal factions.

"They have more than 60 tribes in the country, and they don't talk to each other very well," she says. "So they couldn't figure out their health care problems. … Their main hospitals were in the big cities, but they didn't know what was going on in the local area. He asked if while we were there, we would just see what we could.

"I thought, 'You know, Lord, I came here to go work with kids, and now You're asking me to do something medical and I really don't want to.' But at the end it was really obvious that there were some significant issues in the country with regard to medicine."

Hospitals are not only out of walking range for many Kenyans, but clinics are understaffed and undersupplied. "I watched a young lady eight months pregnant die from hemorrhaging because they didn't have a simple clamp to stop the hemorrhaging. I watched an 8-year-old boy die because they didn't have any sutures. Those things are really tough to see," she says with pain in her voice.

With the government's support and encouragement, a partnership of her local Presbyteries, Hoag Hospital and the local Kenyan government began opening and funding dispensaries, while also providing training to the people who would run them.

"Those dispensaries are flourishing," she says. "We've gone from a 10 percent successful diagnosis rate to about an 80 percent successful diagnosis rate."

What makes this strategy scalable is a focus on equipping the nationals to do the work. "The key thing here is we wanted them to be self-sustaining, we wanted them to offer quality care, and what we were there to do was to train." She points out, "It was a real fight because every place we'd show up there would be 300 to 500 people wanting treatment, and we wanted to train the medical people. So do you go slow and train, or do you treat them, or what do you do? "

Her second-half portfolio includes this type of strategic and leveraged compassion, as well as a much-needed dose of one-on-one compassion. Colette leads teams to Kenya three or four times a year for two or three weeks at a time, and she still makes helping orphans a part of her agenda.

"Every time I'm there I still get up every morning and go play with the kids in the orphanage," she says. "That's still where my passion is, that's what I like to do."

Colette helps with programs and partnerships that focus on orphans, but she never wants to stray too far from the personal. She points out that Jesus "taught 12 people so they could teach others" but always stopped for the individuals who crossed his path.

"The kids we see in Africa sometimes have been abused so much," she says, "they don't even know how to touch, [so we can] give them the gift of touch, love and caring. I can't imagine a world without being able to have that personal side of it."

Colette has a plan-it-build-it-launch-it-release-it model for business and ministry, so there will likely come a day when she'll say goodbye to Kenya. As with the businesses she brainstorms and launches, she wants to see the programs in Kenya grow to the point that they're self-sustaining.

"My last year has been building people to take over and lead the medical trips," she says. "The next thing, we're building people to do the distribution. At some point in time I will no longer be needed. ... There will be a time to move on, and, yes, it will be tremendously sad. I'll probably go crawl into my husband's arms, and have a very good cry, but that's OK."

It will be OK because there will be something else.

"I'm one of those people who believe that you do dream big, and that God is big enough to handle anything and everything," she says. "I love watching God work. I can sit there all day watching what He does, and just thoroughly enjoy and revel in it." HT

For additional information and helpful Web links related to Colette's journey from success to significance, visit www.halftime.org/thesecondhalf and click on her name.

"We've gone from a 10 percent successful diagnosis rate to about an 80 percent successful diagnosis rate."

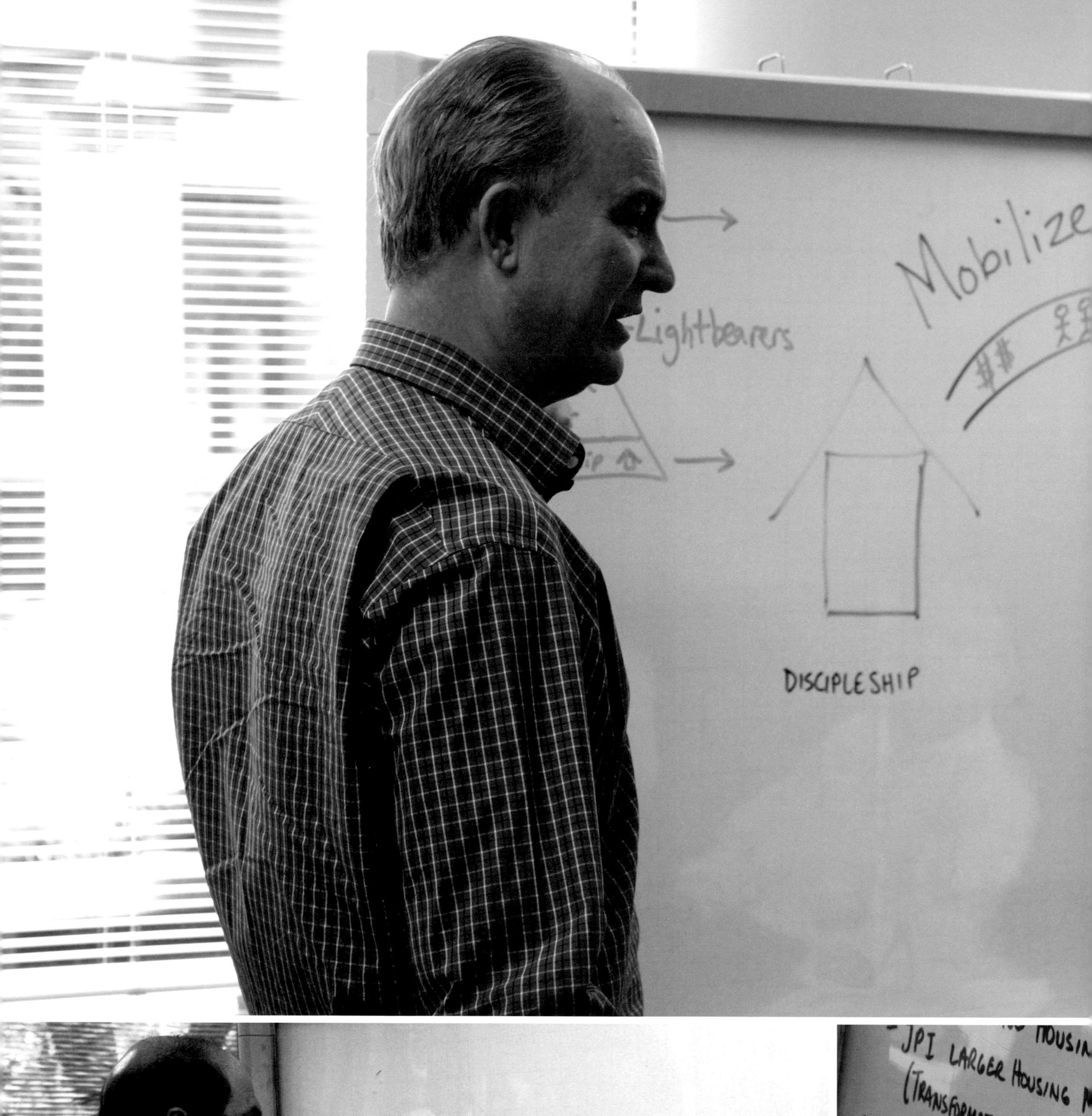

Mobilize
Lightbearers
DISCIPLESHIP

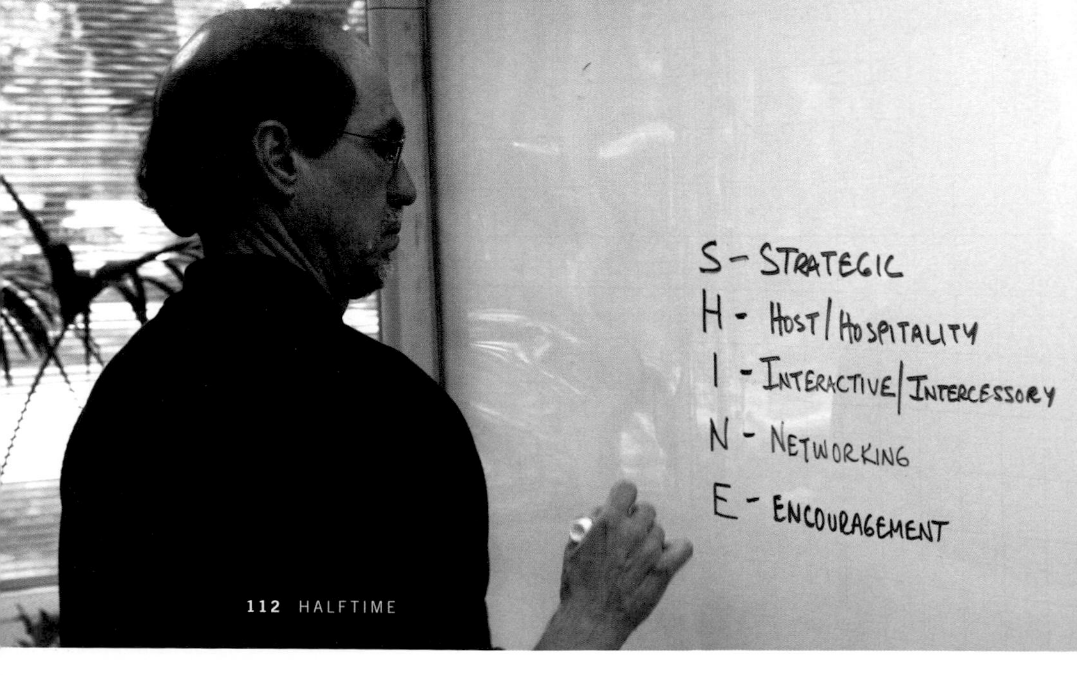

S - STRATEGIC
H - HOST/HOSPITALITY
I - INTERACTIVE/INTERCESSORY
N - NETWORKING
E - ENCOURAGEMENT

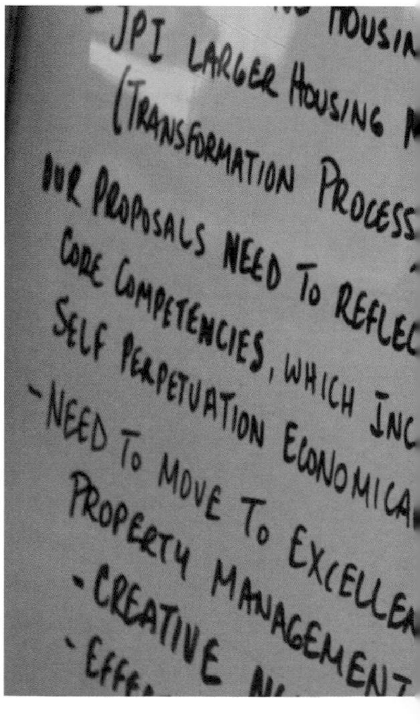
- JPI LARGER HOUSING
(TRANSFORMATION PROCESS
OUR PROPOSALS NEED TO REFLEC
CORE COMPETENCIES, WHICH INC
SELF PERPETUATION ECONOMICA
- NEED TO MOVE TO EXCELLEN
PROPERTY MANAGEMENT
- CREATIVE

Searching for insights

JIM BECKETT

Jim Beckett and Joe Galindo change the world a few hours at a time from a conference room in Dallas.

While many of us settle on a particular project or on working closely with a particular organization, these guys work in staccato bursts with hundreds of organizations and individuals a year. A couple of days a week they invite successful business leaders to help a local ministry think through its business model or a particular challenge it faces. It's an approach that not only deeply impacts nonprofits, but also provides the business leaders with exposure to ministries that can benefit from their talents and it doesn't require giving up their day jobs.

Jim spent his first half building a media company specializing in sports trading cards and collectables. As he explored ministries that caught his attention, he realized that some of them were poised for greatness, but were just missing "that one thing" that they couldn't see, usually because they were too close to the vision, too close to their own organization.

Meanwhile, he noticed that many of his peers were approaching Halftime and were looking "to do something really significant" in their second half but needed exposure to multiple ministries before they found a fit.

He and Joe put together a model in which their business colleagues join them in offering business savvy and consulting skills to nonprofits in their region. The business leaders get the satisfaction that comes from service to others, as well as a broad range of exposure to the work of nonprofits. In the process, they help fading organizations get back on track and startup organizations gain traction.

Including breakfasts, luncheons and retreats that they sponsor, Jim and Joe will participate in hundreds of these strategy sessions in a year. Groups range in size from three or four people to 20; the point is to assemble a small cast of business-savvy leaders who can take in a situation and offer honest, frank advice with no sugarcoating.

"It's a real mix, but almost all of them last about an hour to an hour-and-a-half," Jim says. "It's very short-term, which is how we can get these business guys to show up and weigh in with some of these ministries.

"We're not saying we're omniscient. We're provocative. We're saying, 'Here are some things you may not have thought of. You think you just need more money, but here are some other issues.'"

Jim's unique ability is asking probing questions and distilling strategic insights ("finding order in chaos," as Joe puts it); Joe, meanwhile, sorts through all the ideas and categorizes them on a whiteboard. In less than two hours, something interesting always emerges from the discussions, even if it's not always what the person at the center of it wanted or expected.

"Out of all the meetings we've done, probably 2,000 or 3,000," Joe says, "we'd have a hard time finding five to 10 that were boring. … I think a lot of times people come to get something. We've created a structure where they don't get what it is that they want – whether it's money or whether they want a magic answer – they get more. They get what God wants them to have. That's our objective."

The short but intense discussions take many people outside their comfort zones, Jim says, but that's a great place for seeing things differently, a great place from which to learn.

"They get in that zone of discomfort and all of a sudden their defenses get broken down enough to where they can hear some new truth or some truth they've been discounting," Jim says. "Every person needs encouragement. And they don't all need alteration. But the Christian walk is a team sport, and it's a contact sport. You need your brothers, whether you are in ministry or in business.

"We're going to try to shed some light on it. We're going to try to be encouraging, try to be strategic, intercede for them, but then we're going to trust God for the results."

Ultimately their ministry, which they call SHINE, aims to be provocative, not prescriptive, and as such they are not offended when the collective wisdom of a ministry/individual rejects an idea that they put forward.

Kevin McCollum saw this firsthand when he met with Jim and Joe on a July afternoon in Dallas. Kevin's the executive director of Lightbearers Ministries, a unique discipleship ministry that seeks to "mobilize and connect money, prayer and manpower" to the strategic projects of other ministries around the world.

Lightbearers owns rental properties near several college campuses. The students who live in the houses grow spiritually through intentional discipleship programs, and their rent generates sustainable funds for missions-related projects. With houses serving five different campuses in three states, Kevin and his team believe they now have a proven model that's ready for dramatic growth. So he came to Dallas for a brainstorming session with Jim and Joe.

Very quickly, Jim hit on the idea of partnering with property owners rather than owning every property. It's an idea Lightbearers has considered in the past and now might consider again.

"Jim has proven he has a grasp of business and of how to capitalize on opportunities," Kevin says. "He was looking at this as an opportunity to leverage some things, to take it nationally and reach the most people with the least cost."

"They get in that zone of discomfort and all of a sudden their defenses get broken down enough to where they can hear some new truth or some truth they've been discounting. Every person needs encouragement."

If Lightbearers pursues Jim's idea then Jim's offered to connect the ministry with people he knows who might help in some specific ways, as well as to facilitate more specific discussions. And if Lightbearers passes on that idea? That's fine with Jim. And it won't mean Kevin wasted his time with the meeting.

"It was definitely worth the time," Kevin says. "About two-thirds of the way into it, Jim made it clear we didn't have to use any of this. He said, 'I might give you 10 things to think about and nine of them might not be worth anything, but I hope there's at least one thing that helps.' It was really a pure process. There wasn't a lot of research up front. It was just believers, friends, equals talking things out."

Kevin left encouraged on some fronts and challenged on others. Most of all, he says he saw a pure willingness among Jim and Joe to help, whether it was with ideas or networking or scheduling another meeting somewhere down the road.

"I'm not a deal guy," Jim says. "I'm a consultant, and I have my own kind of facilitating. I like to think through things when I don't have to be the one making deals. That really helps me in not being pushy with some of these people that come. ... We get truthful dialogue out there on the table by the ministry or an individual at a crossroads. I purposely don't tie this to any funding I may or may not do of their ministry. We're just really encouraging these people to consider their options." HT

For additional information and helpful Web links related to Jim's journey from success to significance, visit www.halftime.org/thesecondhalf and click on his name.

Unashamedly ethical

GRAHAM POWER

It's one thing to read about the people God uses to change the world, and it's another to get to know them and to really see inside their world. To share such an experience with one of your children is beyond compare.

It's a Sunday morning, and my daughter Carie and I are visiting Graham Power in Cape Town, South Africa. I've been looking forward to this trip, but not because Graham's one of the most successful contractors and developers in South Africa. My excitement is more because I know my teen-age daughter is meeting a man who built a business on rock-solid ethics and, from that platform, is changing the world in ways both obviously large and seemingly small. Graham's Global Day of Prayer initiative reaches millions of people, but today we'll get a glimpse into the lives of just a few dozen kids.

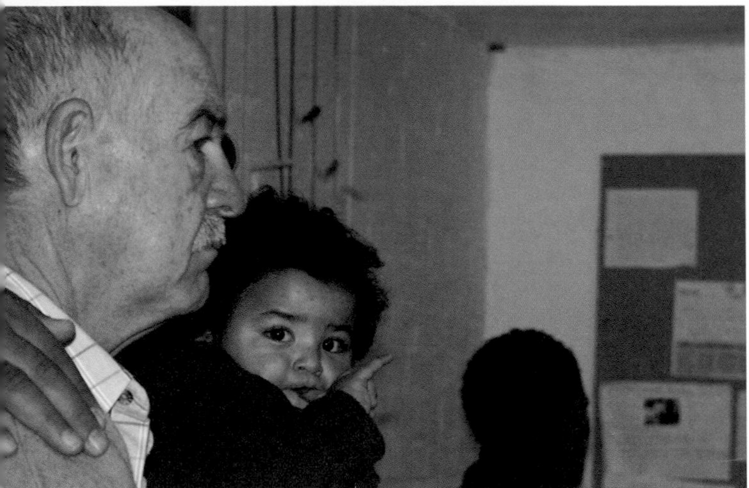

Today he takes us to his farm – the Eagles Rising Center.

And it's some farm.

As we drive in the lane, off to our right is a breathtaking view of False Bay and to the left are towering mountains. With the stiff breeze in our faces, I'm not surprised to learn that this is the windiest valley on the cape. This is where Graham and his wife Lauren lived when they started their family, and the barns out back are where they started their company. Now it's a haven and launching pad for teens who grew up in the black-only ghettos that surround Cape Town called the Townships. (See the Ratcovitch story on page 16)

The farm is home to 38 teens (18- and 19-year olds) for one year while they learn English and business skills so they can be more competitive in the marketplace. The greatest thing the teens are taught is intercessory prayer. The central building on Graham's farm is a 24/7 prayer room where these young Africans pray for the needs of their country and its people.

I could hear the music as we approached, and it was a truly unforgettable experience to walk into a room full of students who were dancing and singing praises to God in Xhosa and Zulu. The energy, the beat and the intensity were captivating. For someone like me with almost no rhythm, it was thrilling to watch them use their feet and bodies to celebrate God. In no time, Carie was swept up in their enthusiasm. You would have thought she grew up with these kids. They are her age and worship the same God, but they have had very different experiences so far in life. This is what I wanted her to see. And as I watch Graham hug one of the boys and whisper a word of encouragement in his ear, I realize this is what I need to see, too.

"These are kids that are growing up in the squatter areas," he says. "They do not know how to use knives and forks. They do not know how to use a flush toilet, and things like that. … They're coming out of the squatter areas where there is no electricity, most of them don't have running water, and there would be six, seven, eight, nine people living in one room. A tin shack [and] when it rains, there are buckets all over just trying to catch the water coming through the roof. And to see how these kids, with a little bit of love and care, can come to have dignity, respect, confidence – that's what's developed."

Graham, who has started 12 different construction/development companies in South Africa, didn't ramp up his commitment to serving God by helping others until a dramatic spiritual experience in 1999 changed the course of his life. As he tried to figure out what the experience meant for his life and work, a pastor from his church gave him a copy of the books *Jesus CEO* and *Game Plan*. Three months into his spiritual journey, Graham read Bob Buford's book *Halftime*.

During this time, God gave him a vision that he viewed simply as an instruction: That Africa would be a light to all nations. Graham's specific calling was to assemble South Africans to repent and pray for forgiveness and reconciliation. Less than a year after his conversion experience, Graham had his first day of prayer in a rugby stadium in South Africa. These 45,000 people consisted of blacks and whites who were not allowed in the same place prior to the abolishment of apartheid. Graham was astonished. "In 102 years since the stadium was built," he says, "it's never been used for anything other than rugby."

In 2001, more than 500,000 people convened in eight stadiums throughout South Africa. Fast forward to 2008 when more than 300 million people prayed in 214 of the 220 identifiable nations in the world.

During our days together, as we drove along the winding coastline, visited the beautiful wineries or sat on his patio

He speaks modestly but frankly about the success of his company, but also about the unseen forces that inevitably shaped his destiny. He doesn't fully understand them, but he doesn't deny them.

overlooking Cape Town, I asked Graham about how all this came to be and about the daunting challenges that face this continent. He doesn't pretend to have all the answers, so he simply tells the stories of what's happened in his life. He speaks modestly but frankly about the success of his company, but also about the unseen forces that inevitably shaped his destiny. He doesn't fully understand them, but he doesn't deny them. They're like the foundations of one of his construction projects – unseen and often unacknowledged by many, but central to the health and survival of the project.

With no formal training, Graham learned about business from the foundation up, and started his first company when he was 28. Power Construction thrived, doubling in size almost every year, adding divisions and eventually becoming known as the Power Group. "I spent my life, from the age of 18 really, just trying to get more business, more wealth," Graham says, "and so my whole life was focused on climbing the ladder." But he lacked true significance until his life changed in 1999.

"We can chase as hard as we like," he says. "We can be the most successful businessperson. We can be making the most money. We can have all the toys in the world. But somehow that void that each of us is born with, well, we will never get an internal peace and calm until we invite Christ into our lives. That I've seen time and time again, and there is no doubt in my mind that none of these other things can fill that void."

When Graham filled that void, his life and work changed dramatically. He made a commitment to running the business with uncompromising ethical standards, even though kickbacks and bribes were common within his industry. His business – which brands itself with the tagline "Unashamedly Ethical" – became a platform for living out his faith.

He tells me the story of a contractor who came into his office because he knew Graham needed to cut back on the number of earth-moving machines he had hired for a project. The contractor offered to pay Graham under the table if he'd keep his equipment on the job. Graham did just the opposite.

"That evening I had all his machines off the project," Graham says, "because, I said, if you come along and you offer that to me, … what are you going to do to one of my junior staff? It's just crazy. So that was my first face-to-face encounter with a direct bribe. I just squashed it on the spot, put the guy off the site, and ever since that encounter I've just been so firm on that issue."

As Graham's company worked on projects across South Africa, he began to see the poverty around him in a different light. That's when he turned the farm into the Eagles Rising Center. Graham sees the future in these teens. He sees them as part of the transformation of Africa, a transformational light to the rest of the world.

"My understanding of a light to the world is not necessarily an economic light to the world," he says. "It may be very different, but I believe that Africa, the Dark Continent, with all its negativity, needs to be turned around. I believe there are a lot of light points, little flickers of light going on."

As I write this story, Carie walks into my office and asks, "What are you working on, Dad?" I tell her I'm writing about Graham. "He's an awesome man!" she says. And as she walks out, I think to myself, "There's one more person who has been deeply impacted by his life. Thanks, Graham." HT

For additional information and helpful Web links related to Graham's journey from success to significance, visit www.halftime.org/thesecondhalf and click on his name.

K YOU! CANA IAN SPONSORS

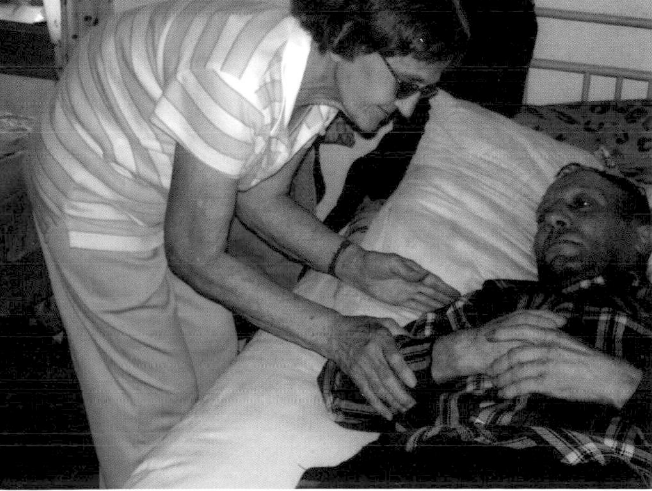

Knee deep in giving

ERNA PENNER

If you're like me, you want a life of significance – not just at midlife, but you want to finish well. At age 84, Erna Penner is not exactly at Halftime, but she sure inspired me when I first met her in Calgary, Canada.

In fact, her story moved me to tears. So I want to share it with you as we wrap up this book.

Her life is what I want my life to look like at age 84.

Erna's life-story is riveting, but what grabbed my heart most is that she is excited about the future – about the women and kids she is serving today. To fully appreciate where she is and where she's going, however, you need to know where she's been.

She was born in 1923 in Ukraine near the Black Sea. Think about it – that was in the aftermath of the Bolshevik Revolution and during a time of brutal Soviet rule that left millions in

Ukraine dead or starving. Her father died when she was three-months-old, and her mother carried out his plan to bring the family to Canada. Finding themselves in a strange country with a strange language, the family battled poverty. And while her two brothers and two sisters married and started families, Erna stayed home and cared for their ailing mother.

When her mother died, Erna, by then 33, enrolled at a university and eventually earned three degrees in education. She taught and served as a principal in Calgary schools until retiring when she turned 65.

That's when she really got going.

"Don't ever retire," she says with a twinkle in her eyes, "it's too busy. I wake up at five o'clock, do all the morning routines, have an early breakfast and dig into my days."

Among other things, Erna's days include organizing efforts to help the poor in Ukraine and speaking to and mentoring women around her home in Calgary.

"You know, your heart gets so full when you can give," Erna says. "And not until you're knee deep can you really experience the joy of giving. ... When you invest in people and look outside your pleasures and your interests – and that doesn't mean to annihilate them – but you know, you get revived totally."

When she retired from the school system, however, Erna wasn't sure what she'd do with her remaining years.

"I got my retirement package, and I was totally at loose ends," she says. "So now what? I have a lot of built in energy. That's a gift. So what do I do? I had no family; I never married."

Then one day she got an e-mail from Lloyd Cenaiko, a successful real estate developer who fell in love with Ukraine while on a trip to trace his family roots. In the mid-1990s, Lloyd founded HART, a nonprofit that supports missions and relief efforts in Ukraine and other parts of Eastern Europe. He wondered if Erna could round up some folks to knit some hats and mittens for poor kids there. As often happens, her second-half calling started out small and grew to serve thousands of kids in Eastern Europe while engaging scores of others in service.

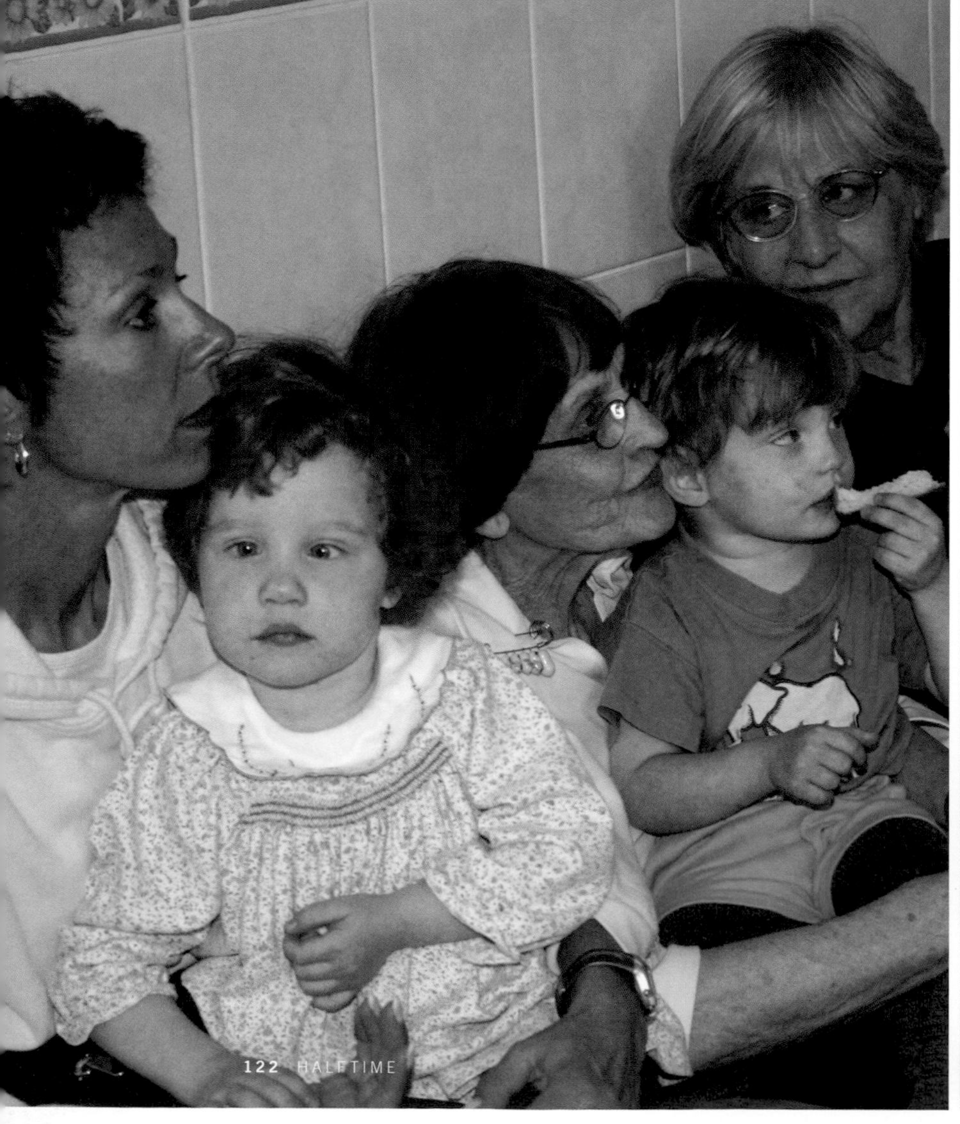

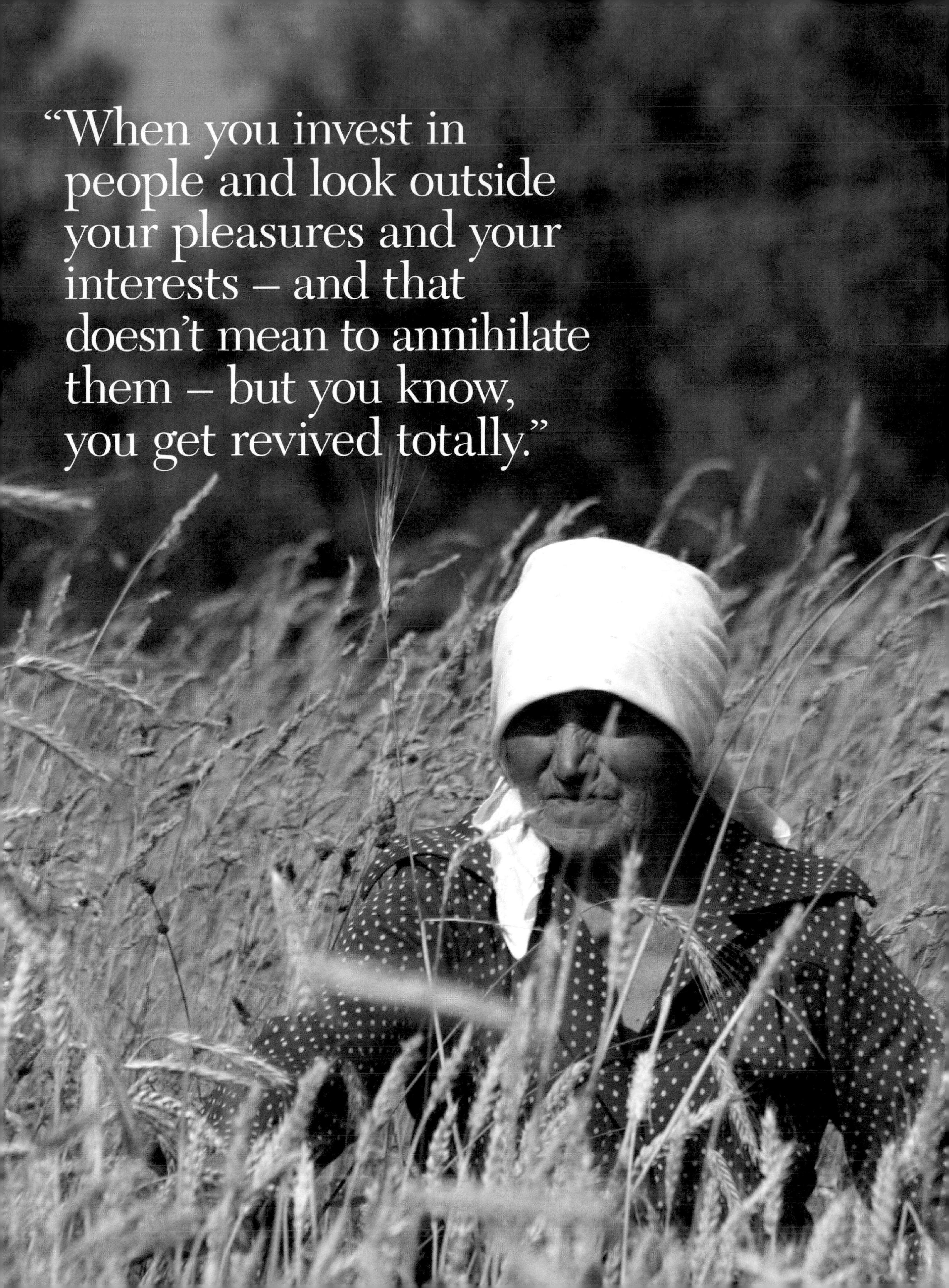
"When you invest in people and look outside your pleasures and your interests – and that doesn't mean to annihilate them – but you know, you get revived totally."

SPORT

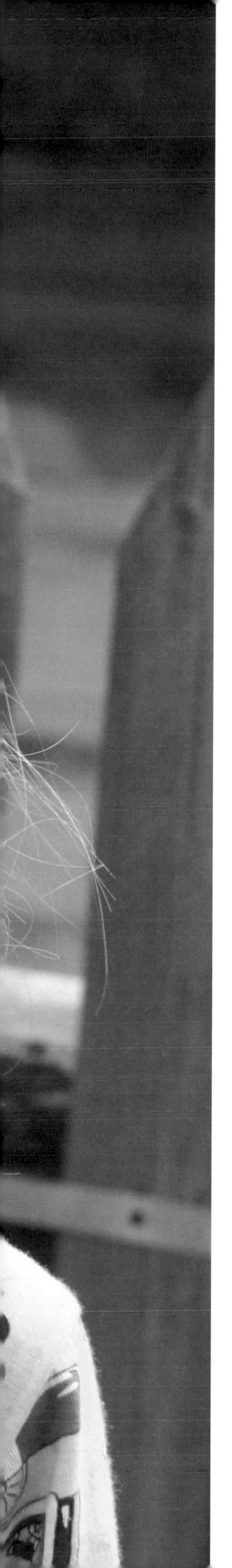

Perhaps her core strength is her ability to get other people to think "beyond themselves."

I wish you could see Erna's eyes as she talks about sending loads of small running shoes (with the little lights that shine when you walk) for those children – it is priceless. Today she's an honorary grandmother to more children than you can shake a stick at – like she said, "God has given me a family like you won't believe."

Using the stories of those poor children, she teaches a unit on Ukraine to elementary students at schools in Calgary, inspiring the next generation to care. Those efforts usually end with a donation drive that yields boxes of shoes, toys and other supplies that are shipped overseas by HART. She also speaks regularly, teaching everything from gardening to practical living skills to coping with singleness. People often stop at her yard to comment on her flowers. So now she teaches gardening to groups of women and uses it as a platform to encourage and mentor them. The seed that Erna planted in my mind (no pun intended) is to look for ways to combine things you love doing that also could serve others.

"My calendar looks like a dog's breakfast," she says with a laugh.

Perhaps her core strength is her ability to get other people to think "beyond themselves." When she speaks to single women, for instance, she reminds them that their identities aren't in their "singleness" but in being children of a living God. "He had a purpose for me, and He has a purpose for you," she tells them. "Let's find it. If God sends a companion across your path, great! And if not, life doesn't stop there."

She inspires groups of women who meet just to socialize to integrate a greater purpose to their time. "Find a purpose outside even your homes or your immediate family, focus on the broader world and let God open the doors," she says. "God opened so many doors for me I don't know which one to walk through first."

Erna no longer struggles with "loose ends."

"So that's my life," she says. "You say, 'Where is your reward?' I tell you, it comes back to me with all the people, my family of God."

Now that's a life-long journey from sacrifice to success to significance – what an inspiration! HT

For additional information and helpful Web links related to Erna's journey from success to significance, visit www.halftime.org/thesecondhalf and click on her name.

Unpacking these stories together.

As I mentioned at the front, this book is designed to help you communicate with your spouse and those around you, folks you love and those impacted by your second-half choices. An important part of getting the most value from the book is asking them to read it, too, and then discussing your individual thoughts and reactions to the stories and what you may have learned. Take an hour and sit down with your spouse or friends after they have read this book and use these questions to help guide your conversation. These questions are carefully written to help you wisely address six big elements of planning your second half.

1. Go briefly through the stories to refresh your memory, and then pick your two favorites. Share with each other what your top two stories are and why.

2. Patrick McConathy (Page 4) followed an unexpected adventure in his second half. What opportunities do you face that might lead to an unexpected second-half adventure? What would give you greater freedom to dream about where they may lead?

3. Linda Hood (Page 52) and Mike Fox (Page 76) are building their second halves on very personal experiences from their past. What circumstances from your first half could provide the impetus and passion for your second half?

4. Paula Dumas (Page 72) and Jeff Stedman (Page 40) look back and see that they were uniquely prepared for their second halves through the training and diverse experiences in their first halves. When you list your experiences, what kind of role(s) might they uniquely equip you for?

5. Rosalind Cook (Page 10) and Dale Dawson (Page 62) discovered something brand new. When Rosalind first put her hands in sculpting clay she knew she was made to sculpt. Dale unexpectedly fell in love with Rwanda. What new experience, place or activity have you been tempted to try that might have similar meaning for your second half? How could you test it out?

6. Dr. Phillip Kemp (Page 58) found that his career already provided the perfect platform to live out his second-half calling. In what ways could your current career serve as a context for your second half? If you pursued those ideas, how would you measure the results differently in your marketplace role?

Your Second Half NEXT STEPS

If the stories in this book touched your heart in a special way, then here are some next steps that might interest you:

1. Share it with others

To help you share these stories with friends, we're making certain quantities of this book available at wholesale prices. Here are some ideas:

> Tell your friends about this book and point them to www.Halftime.org/TheSecondHalf. Word of mouth is still the most effective tool for a book like this to benefit the widest possible audience.

> Give the book to friends. It's a great gift for birthdays or Christmas, and a handwritten note in the front about a story or two that touched your heart will encourage them to open up to the incredible possibilities for their second half.

> Post it on your Web site, Blog and social or professional networking sites. We have a ready-to-use link and description for you to download at www.Halftime.org/TheSecondHalf.

> Put a copy of it in your church library and encourage your church to carry it in its bookstore and mention it on its Web site.

> Present it to your small group or adult Bible study group.

> If you own a company, give it as a gift to employees who are becoming empty nesters or approaching early retirement. If you have clients in midlife, leave a copy in the lobby.

> Give it to clients or suppliers who are successful and who you think might be asking questions about their second half of life.

> If you lead a nonprofit, use this book as a gift to major donors who already give of their money and love your organization but may not have thought about giving their time and talent to share the leadership burden with you.

2. Access other resources for your Halftime journey

Read other books in the Halftime family of books.
Bob Buford's book *Halftime* chronicles his Halftime journey and the lessons he learned along the way. It's the seminal book on this idea, and it was a pivotal part of the lives of many people featured in this book.

From Success to Significance, also written by Lloyd Reeb, provides a roadmap for your journey, including helpful exercises, examples and tips that have made a second half of significance accessible to thousands of people. It is written intentionally for those who may not be financially independent.

Use the *Success to Significance* group curriculum.
This six session video-based curriculum is designed to help you process with your friends what you would like to do with your second half and to create a simple plan to get there. Available at www.successtosignificance.com

Use our online second half planning tools
Access the many online tools that will help you define your core strengths and passions, write a mission statement, create time and margin in life to explore your second-half dreams, and, ultimately, begin to craft your best-fit serving context.

If you don't intend to leave your current career, go to www.successtosignificance.com. If you are financially independent and are open as to how you invest your second half, go to www.halftime.org.

For up-to-date information and ideas on how you can help, go to www.Halftime.org/TheSecondHalf

PHOTO CREDITS

4-9 No Man Left Behind: Partrick McConathy
Dan Coffey Photographics
Select Photos Todd Pinkston, Dallas, TX

10-15 Permission for Passion: Rosalind Cook
Don Kreutzweiser Photography

16-23 A Joint Partnership: Cliff & Rose Ratkovich
Courtesy of HopeBuilders Global &
Tapestry Homes Initiative Ministries
Select Photos Courtesy of Janine A. Swiathkoski
& Rachel Williams

24-27 Connecting the Dots: Dr. David Miller
Courtesy of Dr. David Miller
24 University Building Courtesy of Princeton
Theological Seminary

28-33 Rocking the World: Sandy Griffith
Sissy Gregory Photography

34-39 Surrender Yourself: Bob & Tina Muzikowski
Courtesy of Chicago Hope Academy

40-45 The Sum of it All: Jeff Stedman
Peter Schwepker Photography
40-41 Select Photos Todd Pinkston Dallas, TX

46-51 Ambassador of Compassion: Leo Abdella
Courtesy of Leo Abdella and Christ Fellowship Church Palm
Beach Gardens, FL and stock source

52-57 Finding Life's Pizzazz: Linda Hood
Courtesy of Mercy Ministries of America, Inc.

58-61 Giving the World a Smile: Dr. Phillip Kemp
Courtesy of Dr. Phillip Kemp

62-67 From the Rock to Rwanda: Cavin & Dawson
Courtesy of Dabbs Cavin, Dale Dawson & David Knight
Opportunities International & Bridge2Rwanda Ministries

68-71 Life in the Intersection: Paul Chou
Courtesy of Paul Chou & Junior Achievement China

72-75 Marketing a New Message: Paula Dumas
Andrew Tanner Photography

76-81 Fueling a Passion: Mike Fox
Courtesy of C3 Missions International

82-85 Answering a Rumbling Spirit: Sam Kirk
Courtesy of Youth About Business

86-89 A Simple Idea: Tripp Johnston
Courtesy of SIM/Sports Friends

90-93 Building Into Others: Kemmons Wilson
Murray Riss Photography
90-91 Downtown Memphis Courtesy of Robert Hensley and
stock source
Restaurant Photos Courtesy Rendezvous Restaurant

94-97 All About the Numbers: Gib Vestal
Gil Michael Photography
Select Photos Courtesy of MAM, Memphis Athletic Ministries

98-103 Finding His Priority: Ken Yeung
Courtesy of Ken Yeung Prince of Peace Children's Home

104-107 Living Out Significance: Steve Grism
Courtesy of Springs Church, Winnipeg

108-111 A Portfolio of Compassion: Dr. Colette Cozean
Courtesy of Dr. Colette Cozean

112-115 Searching for Insights: Jim Beckett
Select Photos Todd Pinkston Dallas, TX

116-119 Unashamedly Ethical: Graham Power
Courtesy of Global Day of Prayer & Graham Power
Photos on page 118 Courtesy of Caroline Reeb

120-125 Knee-deep In Giving: Erna Penner
Justin Murphy Photography
Select Photos Courtesy of HART (Lloyd Ceniako)

ABOUT THE AUTHOR

Lloyd Reeb is a successful real estate developer and owner of retirement housing who made a Halftime transition to pursue significance. He is the primary spokesperson for Halftime®, a national ministry that helps people move from success to significance. For more than a decade he has dedicated much of his time to speaking about Halftime issues and coaching individuals who are on this journey.

Lloyd is the author of *From Success to Significance: When the Pursuit of Success Isn't Enough* and co-author of a unique flipbook, *Unlimited Partnership: Igniting a Marketplace Leader's Journey to Significance*, which is a helpful guide to partnering with nonprofit leaders. Lloyd's *Success To Significance Group Curriculum* addresses the needs of people who are not financially independent but still desire to pursue significance in the second half of their lives.

Lloyd, his wife Linda and their three children live in Charlotte, N.C.

For more about Lloyd and his Halftime journey or to interact with him, go to www.halftime.org/thesecondhalf and click on his name.

ACKNOWLEDGMENTS

Special thanks to Greg Murtha for his networking and encouragement and to Jan Hopwood for coordinating this project. Thanks also to Stephen Caldwell for his help with writing and to Daniel Bertalotto of DOXA for their outstanding design.

My friend Laurie Venzon always challenges me to a higher level both in life and in my writing. She did so with this book, for which I'm very grateful.